Holistic Habits

Holistic Habits

Build your best life one small change at a time

Emine Rushton &
Jocelyn de Kwant

Leaping Hare Press

Quarto

First published in 2023 by Leaping Hare Press
an imprint of The Quarto Group.
One Triptych Place, London, SE1 9SH
United Kingdom
T (0)20 7700 6700
www.Quarto.com

A catalogue record for this book is available from
the British Library.

ISBN 978-0-7112-8964-2
Ebook 978-0-7112-8965-9

Illustrations by Pui Lee and Clare Owen
Design by Daisy Woods
Production Manager Maeve Healey

Printed in China
10 9 8 7 6 5 4 3 2 1

Contents

Introduction

What exactly is a habit? Well, it's a regular, embedded tendency – closer to instinct than conscious choice. It could be your specific way of doing something – the order in which you put milk, tea and sugar into your cup, perhaps – or a simple ingrained action, such as brushing your teeth after breakfast or reaching for a glass of wine after work.

These habits form the foundation of our daily lives. They define everything from the routes we take to get to work to the side of the bed we sleep on and, once formed, they're pretty hard to break. This can prove tricky when it's something you're keen to stop doing, but is also very helpful if you're looking to invite a whole new wave (or just a few regular micro-moments) of positive change into your daily life.

Habit formation is also the area of some fascinating emerging behavioural science with people such as James Clear (author of *Atomic Habits*) analysing what enables people to form solid routines and daily infrastructures, and then helping them to be more productive and successful as a result. What's interesting, is that once a habit sticks, it requires very little thought. But the initial formation of the habit is the opposite – it's a choice and, through the continual, consistent choosing of that choice, we create a pattern that's hard to break.

The realm of this book is the multiple, marvelous ways you might begin to enjoy the present-moment a whole lot more — with new ideas, activities and reflections, which then flow into the natural formation of happy, healthy holistic habits that really stick.

The expansive, evolving playfulness of the journey you're about to take is THE whole point. We're not here to get you all fixated on final destinations and stressed out about to-do lists. We have enough of that relentless pressure in our lives without inviting it into this book too!

So, instead of daily ticks and trackers and dated tasks (and consequently beating yourself up if you miss a week or do something in the wrong order) we've divided *Holistic Habits* up into twelve chapters, so that you have a whole month to explore a new habit 'focus' with thirty days' worth of supportive ideas, exercises and activities to really get you walking the talk.

And it all begins with the upfront work of consciously choosing what lovely things you'd like to invite in on a regular basis, and then — the even more fun bit! — getting to explore the inventive, exciting and enriching ways to root them into your daily life.

James Clear writes about the four triggers of successful habit formation — Cue, Craving, Response and Reward. So, in order to create habits that stick we have to initially feel inspired by an idea and really want to experience it, before then acting on that impulse, and ultimately enjoying the result. It sounds simple, and in a lot of ways it is, but the real key to creating and enjoying healthy new habits, is to embrace changes that nourish more than just one part of your life.

That's why we've called this book *Holistic Habits* — because the rewards you'll gain from trying the 350+ ideas across these pages are manifold and designed to benefit you as a whole – mind, body, heart and soul. This isn't just about thinking differently either – it's about making supportive, interconnected choices that FEEL amazing – everything from building towards a better night's sleep to decluttering your home.

And rather than getting bogged down in the unhelpful habits that need a nip in the bud, here, in the happy realm of *Holistic Habits*, we're focusing solely on the choices we want to consciously adopt and enjoy; creating healthy patterns that not only stick, but uplift, inspire, support and empower.

The fact is, it all shifts the moment you decide to take action (that's the Response part of the habit formation cycle) because it's not enough to inwardly reflect and set intentions, we actually have to follow through in order to reap the benefits. And by taking that same enjoyable action, day after day, you're building unbreakable bridges between the healthy intentions you're setting and the habits you're forming.

The best part? You get to decide where your journey begins and ends. You may want to start this book by reading through the different chapters and going where your heart takes you. You may land on one specific idea and decide that you want to repeat it daily until you've rooted a whole new healthy holistic habit into your life for good. Or you may view an entire chapter as the ideal opportunity to support yourself in a key life change (for example, getting out into nature more, or adding more mindful movement into your day).

You may also want to work through the book in the order it's been created — a purposeful balance between the more playful and reflective offerings — and spend a month on each for a year-long experience. Or you may want to dip in and dip out in ways that suit you and your life better. It's your life and your choice!

Wherever you land within this book, and whatever direction you choose, we hope you'll find the enriching suggestions practical, sustainable and pleasurable. And remember — every moment offers us the fullest potential for a fresh start, so there's never any better place to start than right here, right now: one small but steady step at a time, towards life-long habits that support and nourish you, each and every day.

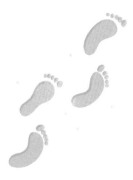

Preparation
Exercises

It can be really helpful to step away from the everyday for just long enough to get our thoughts and feelings in order. To sit and reflect. To reprioritise. To clarify our values and how they inform our choices. Often, if we think back to childhood, we remember a more leisurely time... ample opportunities to watch ants crawl, clouds shift, stars wink and dance. And perhaps with that free space and time (something we might once have called 'boredom') we might also have found fresh new ways to understand the world around us, and to unravel the unending wooly notions we were forming about our place within it, too. These formative experiences were just that — foundation-building — and taught us precious lessons about observation, stillness and problem-solving. Who doesn't feel better for an hour spent among the trees, or a quiet, solitary walk in the park, letting our feelings ebb and flow, until something completely new emerges in the place where confusion or overwhelm once lived? When we think of forming new healthy, holistic habits then, it can be helpful to think about the choices that lead us to feelings of expansion and curiosity. What is it we are doing or experiencing when we have our big lightbulb moments; when do we feel most playful and inventive? When we do feel most inspired and alive? These are the feelings that can guide us well — like arrows shot direct from the heart, which is often our best compass. These opening exercises were created to offer just this sort of opportunity — a bit of breathing space, with an in-built invitation to consider the foundations upon which you might like to build, one small step at a time.

1

Write your name down the side of this page. Now create an acrostic by starting a new word with each of the letters in your name. Choose skills and traits to celebrate – for example, MIA: MUSICAL; INVENTIVE; ARTISTIC.

2

If you could live your life by any motto, what would it be? Ask yourself what's stopping you.

....

....

....

....

....

....

3

Describe a moment you hope to celebrate in the future.

....

....

....

....

....

....

4

Ponder this question for a while: how do I live life as fully as possible?

5

Spiritual teacher Eckhart Tolle said that we are more motivated to awaken from a nightmare than from a pleasant dream, and that 'evolution occurs in response to a crisis'. Think about unhelpful patterns or habits you wish to change. What will you do about them?

CHAPTER 1

Rise & Shine

Life is a series of eternal cycles... birth to death, new moon to full, sunrise to sunset. When we rise each morning, that morning's momentum and energy are defined by the night that came before... and, in turn, the flavour of the day ahead is inextricable from the mood of the morning we enter into. Mornings have long been my favourite time of the day. There is something so delicious about being up first... about moving into the day with a sense of purpose... about choosing to seek goodness, nourishment and enjoyment before most others have shaken off sleep; of coming into the day with gentleness: no alarm, no rush, no fuss. When we wake with kindness — giving ourselves enough time to come fully to our senses, nourishing ourselves with a good first meal, hydrating our parched systems with herbal tea or warm water, awakening all of our senses by stepping outside to greet the sun and sky and forgoing the urge to dive immediately into emails and obligations, we dramatically raise the odds of the rest of the day going well. We remind ourselves that we do have a say in how we enter our day. We remember that joy is intrinsic to living and more readily found and felt when not buried beneath a mountain of morning tasks, trials and tribulations. When we peel back the edge of those first moments of each day, we find a window of opportunity... a window we get to fill with gentleness and joy.

1

Each morning, before you do anything at all — before you even
open your eyes or begin to move — find three reasons to be thankful
for this new day. From the song of the birds to the softness of your
pillow, hold on to your three reasons until you REALLY feel them.
Then, and only then, get ready to wake up and greet the day.
Make a note of your three reasons here.

1 ....

2 ....

3 ....

2

Different cultures greet the day in different ways, and a simple
'good morning' is a very jolly thing to say each day, when you
come to think of it. If you could greet the day in your own way,
what would you say?

....

....

....

....

....

....

....

3

Make a morning steeper: simply pop apple and/or pear slices and a cinnamon stick into a flask of hot water for delicious hydration to comfort you on your way to work. Naturally sweet flavours are soothing; imagine you're replenishing your inner cup as you drink, and take the time to breathe in the fragrant fruit and spice steam with each sip.

4

Greet your morning face in the mirror without fear or judgement. Smile at your reflection, gently lay your hands on your skin and embrace your uniquely natural beauty.

5

Making the bed in the morning should be a slow ritual, not a rushed chore. Take time to smooth, fold, straighten, shake out and refresh your bed. Place your pillows and blankets just as you like them. What one thing will you leave on your bedside table, ready to welcome you later in the day? Squiggle it down here.

6

Swap an alarm for a gentler start to the day. If you have blackout blinds or very thick curtains, a daylight lamp is a good option. It mimics sunrise, with its light gently building to coax you out of sleep.

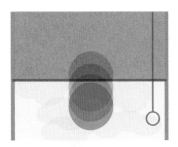

7

What's the first thing you want to see when you wake up in the morning? Sketch it here.

8

It's always lovely to rise to the promise of a delicious breakfast. Think of what you'll need to pick up at the shop or market today, in order to enjoy your favourite breakfast tomorrow.

9

Between 6 a.m. and 9 a.m. sunlight is at its most healing and safe. Your body absorbs precious vitamin D without the risk of heightened UV exposure. Morning sun boosts your happy hormone serotonin and your natural feel-good endorphins, and even lowers blood pressure. Try to reorganise your mornings so that you have time to sit outside for a short spell (weather permitting).

10

Morning movement helps wake up your muscles and nerve endings, your brain and joints. Try a short round of sun salutations — gentle yoga stretches that get the blood and heart pumping.

11

Each day of the week has its own unique 'flavour'... slow and steady or muddled and manic. Colour in your dream week here, using a different colour for each day. Let your imagination run wild and free, envisioning each day just as you would like it to be: full of technicolour wonder.

Monday

Tuesday

Wednesday

Thursday

Friday

Saturday

Sunday

12

Everyone should have a good morning playlist. Think about the ten happiest songs that make you tap your toes, wiggle your bottom and grin from ear to ear. Pop them into a playlist and, whenever your morning feels grey, press play.

13

Slide a picture of a joyous memory into your bag or purse. Make time to look at it every morning on your way to work. Let the happiness fill you up.

14

Overnight oats are the simplest way to prep a delicious breakfast in advance. Simply half-fill a clean jar with oats, cover them with the milk or yoghurt of your choice and add your toppings. Lid on, pop in the fridge. In the morning, stir through, add some fresh fruit on top and you're good to go! Here are some yummy combinations to inspire breakfast time:

Oats + peanut butter + honey
/ top with banana

Oats + vanilla + cacao + brown sugar
/ top with blueberries

Oats + cinnamon + honey
/ top with strawberries + desiccated coconut

15

Create your own motto using a few powerful words that make you feel confident and optimistic. Write them on a piece of paper that you can pop into a small frame to keep by your bedside. Write your motto down here, too.

16

When you wake up with natural sunlight, the light waves immediately boost your alertness, brain function and mood – ironically, the stuff many of us ordinarily drink coffee to 'feel'. Take this book outside before breakfast and colour in the sun as it appears in the sky today.

17

If the first thing you do when you wake up in the morning is smile, you are already on the right foot. Even if you don't feel like getting up, smiling can help convince your brain that you do. What's the one thing that is guaranteed to make you smile? Stick in a picture or prompt here, ready for the morning.

18

If your system feels sluggish and slow in the morning, enjoy some grated fresh ginger and a slice of lime or lemon in a mug of hot water, at least thirty minutes before breakfast.

19

Keep a comfort read by your bed, one filled with uplifting short passages or reflections. Take just one minute each morning to open your book at random and read from it. Make this positive practice part of your purposeful morning routine.

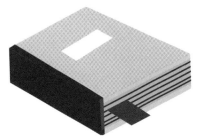

20

Open your wardrobe and pull out the first item of clothing your heart is drawn to. Wear it today!

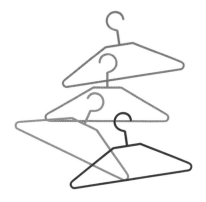

21

Instead of living by your to-do list, reclaim joy with a daily love list. For each day, list one new activity or experience to look forward to. It can be as simple as enjoying a slice of cake and a cuppa in the garden, or taking the first step towards a bigger project, such as learning a new language, or trying a new craft. Write your seven-day love list here.

Monday

Tuesday

Wednesday

Thursday

Friday

Saturday

Sunday

22

Pick a favourite outdoor spot and zoom in on one tiny patch of it early in the morning. Observe the flowers and insects, sounds and smells. Revisit the same spot at sunset. How is it different? What has changed the most? What remains the same?

23

Eminently enlivening, rosemary is a great head clearer. Keep a generous fresh sprig hanging from the showerhead in the bathroom, for instantaneous energy-boosting steam.

24

Carry a little comfort around with you, even when far from home. From a small protective crystal to a favourite aromatherapy spray, sketch your home-comforts-to-go in this protective pouch.

25

Before you start your day, take a quiet moment to go outside in your bare feet and get in touch with the temperature outside. Feel the ground under your soles. Take a couple of deep breaths, inhaling the morning air. Make some notes about what you see, hear and feel.

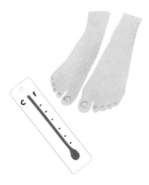

26

You needn't wait until New Year to set your intentions and resolutions. The simple act of choosing a word for the day can help you get clear on what it is you want to feel and achieve. Etch your word into this calendar each morning for a week. Every time you lose your way, repeat the word in your mind to create both clarity and purpose.

27

Some of the best dreams are the simplest ones. Set yourself five tiny, everyday wishes and hopes to remind yourself of the joyful, generous potential within ready reach. Make a list of your wishes here.

1 ....

2 ....

3 ....

4 ....

5 ....

28

The sound of birds singing as loudly as they can just before sunrise is known as the 'dawn chorus'. Due to the lack of wind in those pre-dawn hours, female birds can better identify the different males, because each has a unique song. The male birds might also be trying to prove they are the toughest by being able to sing so energetically so early in the morning. If you get the chance, wake up with the dawn chorus.

29

Instead of a to-do list, make a to-don't list for today. Think of things you normally do despite your feelings about them, things that are plain annoying, or maybe not that important. Add them to your to-don't list and simply don't do them today. Indulge yourself!

To Don't

....

....

....

....

30

Keep a pot of fresh mint or lemon verbena on your kitchen windowsill. Pop a few fresh leaves into a cup of hot water for a vitalising and aromatic morning brew. Enjoy it somewhere quiet, even if just for a few moments.

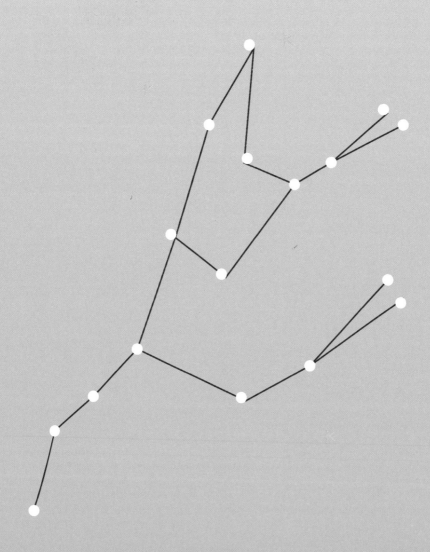

CHAPTER 2

Unwind & Sleep

Long before the age of technology, nighttime was known only as the land of nod: once the sun set and the sky fell dark, all work and activity necessarily ceased, and the more restful part of the day began. Today, with endless sources of artificial light and their accompanying stimulation, we have moved further and further away from our natural body clocks and circadian rhythms. As a result, many of us struggle to sleep well, and yet we are wired to do just that – to rise with vim and gusto, and slumber with ease and depth. It's time to start slowly moving our body clocks a little closer to their natural rhythms, taking our lead from the natural world around us, generous in its hints and clues as to how, when and why we should prepare ourselves for sleep. And indeed, when we choose to 'prepare' for sleep, we accept that sleep often requires a little laying of the groundwork – from the repetition of easeful melodies to the lulling calm of mantras, soothing teas and somniferous scents. There is also a need to reflect back on the day that has passed – to collect the treasures and store them away for another time, knowing that once down on paper, they need no longer be carried around in the mind. When we approach our nights as we approach our days – with clear, quiet intention – things unfold just as they should... just as nature intends.

1

Spend a month marking up your very own moon map. From new moon to full moon, jot down your thoughts and feelings each night, for twenty-eight days. You may want to photocopy these pages so you can carry on using them, month after month.

Notes:

....

....

....

....

....

....

....

....

....

....

....

....

....

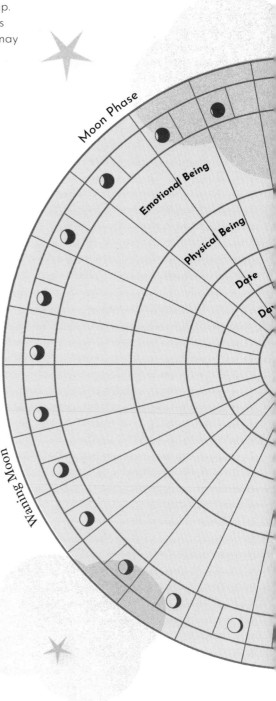

Waxing Moon

Start Date:

....

End Date:

....

2

Once upon a time, we would have lain to sleep with the sunset and risen with the sunrise. To regulate our sleep patterns today, in this 'always on' world, the best thing we can do is stick to a regular rising and sleeping time. What are the ideal times for you to get into bed, to fall asleep, to wake up and to begin your day? Sketch your intentions on the clock.

3

Mark the bridge between work and home with a scent. Before stepping over the threshold of your home – particularly if the day has been long and trying – slow down, breathe deep and reach into your coat pocket. Keep something fragrant there – cardamom pods, for example. Take a couple, crush them, breathe the earthy aroma and feel ready to step inside.

4

Blue light from electronic devices has been shown to interfere with the body's melatonin production – and we need melatonin to begin our sleep-inducing cycle. Get out your diary – on which nights of the week can you realistically commit to a screen curfew, ideally two hours before bedtime?

5

Yoga nidra, or yogic sleep, is one of the most restorative practices available to us. The simple process of lying down, warm and comfortable, while following a gentle, guided meditation, beautifully unfurls the body and mind. Find one you like from the countless meditation apps and free downloads available.

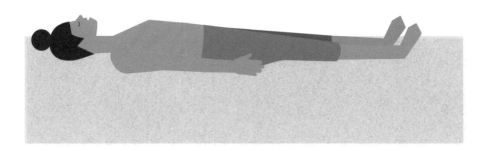

6

'Lulla' and 'bye' — these two words were combined in the 1500s to make the 'lullaby' that we now sing to our children. But lullabies soothe the singer, too. Pen some simple words of your own to bring calm to the end of your day, and set them to your favourite gentle tune. Write your lullaby here.

....

....

....

....

....

7

Think about the things that soothe you the most. A mug of cocoa? The smell of lavender? A loving cuddle? Come up with ten things and have fun inviting them into your nighttime wind-down routine. Aim to enjoy at least one every evening. Write your list here.

1 ....

2 ....

3 ....

4 ....

5 ....

6 ....

7 ....

8 ....

9 ....

10 ....

8

'Legs up the wall' is, officially, the most relaxing yoga pose of all. Colour in these lovely legs, before going off to enjoy some limbo-limb time yourself.

9

Two of the most powerful mantras you can repeat to yourself at bedtime are...

'I give myself permission to rest.'

'Nothing is needed of me right now.'

Try these when you are struggling to relax. Add a third mantra of your own to the mix — one that really resonates with you.

10

Writing down your thoughts and feelings at the end of each day is a wonderful way to clear the mind and clean the slate ahead of sleep. Use this page to jot down the very first words that rise up into your mind the moment you put your pen to the paper. Don't judge the words that rise up — simply let them flow out. Once written, release them from your mind.

11

Look up the times of the sunset for the next week. Make a gentle commitment to yourself to down tools at sunset if you can, and have an offline evening, with no screens at all. Jot the times down here.

Monday

....

Tuesday

....

Wednesday

....

Thursday

....

Friday

....

Saturday

....

Sunday

....

12

Can you remember a favourite bedtime story from childhood? What was it called? What characters were in it? Any lines you recall? Jot them down in your own storybook, as a reminder of nighttime's peaceful promise and potential.

13

Name one enjoyable thing you had hoped to do today, but did not find the time for. How long would it have taken? Plan this exact amount of time into your diary for the coming week, and do it.

14

At the end of the day your mind may feel a little like the active windows on your desktop computer — left with a hundred tabs open. Imagine that you have the ability to bookmark, save and then shut down those tabs. List the four most pressing thoughts you have, one by one. Once you've finished, say out loud: 'I am now shutting down.'

1 ....
2 ....
3 ....
4 ....

15

'Urgent' is a matter of life or death. It is act now, or else. Yet we mark our emails with the word, and letters stamped with it regularly fly through our letterboxes. This is because we are hardwired to act when something truly IS urgent. Companies take advantage of this and use it to get our attention. Let's take that power back. Spend a few minutes thinking about the things you have labelled 'urgent' that are not, in fact, a matter of life or death. Add them to the 'Not Actually Urgent' list.

Not Actually Urgent

....
....
....
....
....
....
....

16

Twilight is that most magical time of day when the sun has just slipped below the horizon, bringing an ethereal glow to the earth. Set an intention to sit and watch the sunset, then twilight.

17

One of the most common places for us to hold tension is in the jaw. Try some facial yoga to loosen up the mandible. Simply open up your mouth as wide as it will go and then close your mouth again, before pretending to blow out a candle. Do this three-step sequence twenty times each night before bed. It will leave your jaw comfortably slack and soft.

18

Rubbing your eyes when tired stimulates the lacrimal gland, which lubricates and soothes the eyes. It also stimulates the muscles that move the eye and this reflex in turn slows the heart, which, some studies suggest, leads to a feeling of relaxation. Use relaxing swirls to fill in these eyes... the repetitive circle has been found to be one of the most soothing to look at. Some say it is even... hypnotic...

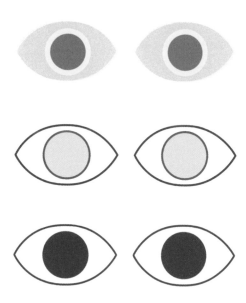

19

When was the last time you swam in the sea? Numerous studies have shown that sea swimming reduces stress and insomnia, while also increasing longevity and holistic wellbeing. Mimic the benefits with a briny bath. Add two big cups of sea salt to the tub, sink in and let your mind sail away.

20

Lavender makes a wonderful fragrant, sleep supporting tea. Plant up a little pot and pluck a few flowers to steep in hot water to drink before bedtime. Come late summer, cut the flowering heads back to the base of each stem and dry the flowers in a sunny spot, spread over a tea towel. Jar the dried purple heads to keep you in plentiful sleepy tea until the following summer.

21

Don't forget to keep your feet warm! In traditional Chinese medicine, the health of the heart is linked to the warmth of the feet. Enjoy a nightly warm foot spa: add herbs and salt to a large bowl, and fill with hot water. Afterwards, cosy your toesies up in your softest socks.

22

Sliding into a freshly made bed is eminently joyful, and studies have shown that seventy-three per cent of us sleep better in clean sheets. Make a point of changing your sheets every week – both your senses and your sleep will thank you for it.

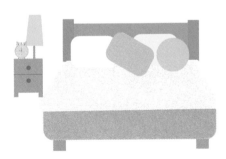

23

Before artificial lighting, there was little more to do than reflect, talk and sleep after the sun had set. Things changed a lot after the invention of the lightbulb. People started to move daytime activities into the night. Since then, we've started to miss valuable hours for reflection. Today, don't turn the lights on just yet. Reflect on the day, alone or with someone, and go to bed the moment you feel tired. Write about the experience.

24

Go on an evening stroll with a friend just after sunset. Don't talk, set your phone to silent mode, and walk more slowly than you usually would. Inhale deeply. What do you smell and what sensations and emotions do you feel?

25

Whenever you can, sleep with the window open, using earplugs when there is too much noise. A cool bedroom is one of the best ways to get a good night's sleep, and feeling the breeze at night will help you sleep like a baby. In children's nurseries in many Nordic countries, they often let the babies and toddlers nap outside – under warm blankets, of course.

26

Did you know that trees sleep at night? Finnish researchers found that trees relax their branches at night, which they saw as a sign of snoozing. The researchers observed the branches and leaves of silver birches, and found that they sagged up to 10 cm (4 inches) at night. They perked up again just before sunrise. Because the branches lifted up before the sun was up, the researchers concluded that the trees rely on their own internal circadian rhythm. Take an evening stroll and keep an eye open for the night trees. Do you see the branches sagging a little? Close your eyes and visualise yourself as a tree. Feel your roots growing into the ground, grounding you. Hold your head up high and as steady as a wise old tree. And just like a tree at night, relax every muscle in your body by dropping it a little. Let go of any tension.

27

The night has inspired many poets, writers and musicians. Let yourself be inspired by the night and compose a little poem, or just let your pen write down the feelings you associate with the night. Not a writer? Search for lyrics and quotes about the night and copy them here.

28

Rediscover your biological clock. Organise an evening without screens and social events and dim the light. Notice when you start to feel tired or cold, a sign that your body is preparing for sleep. Go to bed as soon as you feel sleepy, without checking your phone or putting on an alarm clock. What time did you go to bed? At what time do you wake up? How many hours did you sleep? Try this a couple of times to see how many hours you sleep when nature takes its course. Try to sleep that number of hours every night.

29

The reassuring sounds of waves or meandering streams are said to help us fall asleep and stay asleep. Listen to a recording of relaxing water sounds and note what it does to your mood.

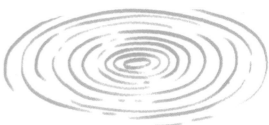

30

Andrew Weil is an American doctor who invented the 4-7-8 exercise, which helps to encourage sleep. It's simple. Breathe in silently for four seconds, hold your breath for seven seconds, and breathe out through your mouth for eight seconds, making a 'whoosh' sound. Repeat four to eight times. It will help you relax quickly.

CHAPTER 3

Natural Connection

Living inside with double glazing and central heating, the electric lightbulb and the Internet, it's quite possible to forget that the elements even exist on the other side of the door. But exist they do — and by making just a little more time to bear witness to the daily rise and fall of the sun, waxing and waning of the moon, cloud formations and constellations, we access a wholly free passport to a world of beauty and inspiration. A moment in nature is never wasted — the natural world all around us is a living, breathing harmony, abuzz with activity, purpose and inspiration — and studies confirm that by spending just two hours every week (as little as seventeen minutes a day), we significantly improve our holistic health and wellbeing. This chapter is therefore filled with the simplest ideas to tap you back into nature's wisdom and wonder — whether spending a restful evening tuning into the nocturnal natters of your garden, or turning a drab day on its head with a colour hunt on the way home. The more you embrace the free and abundant opportunities on your own doorstep, the more deeply you'll embed your daily nature habit — and soon enough, you'll find yourself itching for your fix of sky, stars, birds and flowers, and may even find that you pick up some creative new hobbies along the way, from flower pressing to bark rubbing. And for those whose time is at a premium or aren't easily able to access the natural world, we've also found clever ways to invite the outside in — all proven to lift the mood and help root a healthy natural habit into the every day.

1

When we are in nature, we often remain so consumed with our thoughts that we miss the tiny details. Nature journalling is a wonderful way to develop the art of really SEEING. The next time you head out, take your journal with you. Collect fallen leaves, flowers to press, bark to etch. Find the time to write an entry in your journal each time, too.

2

Earthing isn't an alien concept. When we stand barefoot on the ground, the soles of our feet absorb earth's faint electromagnetic frequencies. This deeply de-stressing exchange is simple and free – all you need to do is take off your shoes.

3

What we hear when we are in nature is as intrinsic to the relaxing experience as what we see, smell and touch. Why not replicate this by creating a nature soundscape from the thousands of downloadable tracks available online? Choose all of your favourite sounds – birdsong, ocean, wind, rain – and have it playing in the background at home, or while you work.

4

For a sunny day: in the morning, turn your head to face the sun and close your eyes. Repeat this at around noon and in the evening. Notice the difference in the intensity and warmth. What is the effect of the sunlight on your face? Describe the feeling.

....

....

....

....

5

Although we talk about four seasons, ecologists actually distinguish six. The prevernal season is when tree leaf buds begin to swell. You can smell that spring is coming, but it's not actually here yet. We know the vernal season as spring. This is when the buds burst open to reveal leaves. The peak of summer, when the trees are in full leaf, is called the aestival season. During the serotinal season, the leaves begin to change colour. In the autumnal season, the leaves start to fall. In the hibernal season, the trees are bare and the leaves begin to decay. Write down five observations on what is typical of the season at this time of year where you live. They can be related to plants, the weather or wildlife.

1 ....

2 ....

3 ....

4 ....

5 ....

6

The sounds of nature at night are known for their relaxing powers. Even when there is traffic noise in the background, noticing natural sounds can help you to relax. Focus on the crickets, frogs, owls, and other nocturnal birds, the fluttering sounds of flying bats on a search for food, and rustling leaves in the wind. Note or draw what you hear.

....

....

....

....

....

....

7

If you cannot easily get away from the digital world, imbue your screen time with influences from the natural world. Studies have shown that even looking at digital images of nature relaxes us.

8

Make nature microbreaks a daily habit. Research at the University of Melbourne in Australia showed that even a thirty-second microbreak looking at a green roof gave subjects a creativity boost. Do you work next to a window? Make it a routine that every time you press 'send' on an email, you look outside for at least thirty seconds. It will give your brain a well-deserved break after a moment of focus.

9

It's always possible to have a brief connection with nature, even when walking down the street. For example, look for a fallen tree leaf. Pick up one that attracts you in some way, perhaps a tiny leaf that has fallen off prematurely or one with beautiful colours.

10

Restore the wonderment that is so easily lost in the hustle and bustle of our busy lives. Look at a natural object in your urban surroundings and open your mind and your heart. Wonder about something. What questions come to mind?

11

City trees are strong trees and they are important to the environment. They improve air quality, cool down the streets, regulate water flow, reduce carbon emissions, lift the spirits of city people — the list goes on and on. Find a big city tree. Smell it. Guess its age. Some trees are so old they have seen the city without cars, before it was even a city. Place your hand on the tree and wonder about everything it has seen.

12

Even in the midst of a busy city, you can find moss growing, like tiny green oases in a concrete desert. Some kinds of moss look like a miniature forest when you observe them with a magnifying glass. Try to find different types of mossy landscapes today.

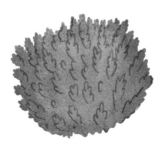

13

People feel less benefit from a natural area where there is a lot of litter. Is the park near your house swarming with plastic waste? Organise a neighbourhood cleanup! It has three benefits: you'll enjoy a cleaner environment (at least for a while); physical activity for the community will leave you feeling satisfied and content, especially as it's an outdoor activity; plus, it will foster positive relationships with your neighbours.

14

To adapt to the changing of the seasons from summer to autumn, then winter, without the sad feeling that sometimes accompanies the fewer hours of sunlight, it helps if we spend as much time as we can outside. Think of smart ways you can spend more time outdoors. Get off at an earlier bus stop and walk the rest of your journey. Spend your breaks outside. Avoid tunnels and choose to travel or do things outdoors whenever you can.

15

What might look at first like a boring overgrowth of neglected plants alongside a road can become something much more interesting when you take a closer look. Focus on a piece of nature you would usually pass by without noticing. Find something about it that intrigues you. Take a photograph and draw it.

16

Even if we feel removed from nature because we are surrounded by brick and concrete, the sky is always there. Take a sky-watching break today and draw what you see above the rooftops.

17

You might not think it, but cities are unexpected havens for birdwatchers. Berlin, Germany has the largest urban population of goshawks in the world, and in Central Park, in New York City, you can see some rare birds, especially during migration season. Look for birdlife in your hometown. They may be nesting on chimneys or swooping through the trees in parks. Watch a big tree to see which birds fly in and out of its branches. Keep an eye open for loose feathers on the ground. If you find one, paste it here.

18

Take your daily break outside today. Bring a cup, thermos, or flask filled with your favourite brew. Drink it somewhere outdoors, preferably underneath trees. Drink it mindfully and notice the nature around you.

19

Trees in the forest have a way of spreading their branches in the sky, so they protect the earth from drying out because of sunlight. The result is a beautiful, crochet-like blanket of green over our heads, with golden sunrays filtering through. The Japanese have a particular word for sunshine that filters through the leaves of trees: *komorebi*. Look up and see how the tree branches spread. Take a photograph to capture it.

20

An exciting way to enjoy the wild is to look for signs of animals. Act like a ranger and make field observations. Search near water, in particular, and along smaller side trails. Look for droppings, nests, eggs, feathers, scratch marks and signs of feeding, such as empty snail shells or piles of seed pods. Record your observations by drawing or writing here.

21

Go out on a colour hunt. Find natural objects that match the colours
shown on this page. Draw or glue them next to their corresponding colours.

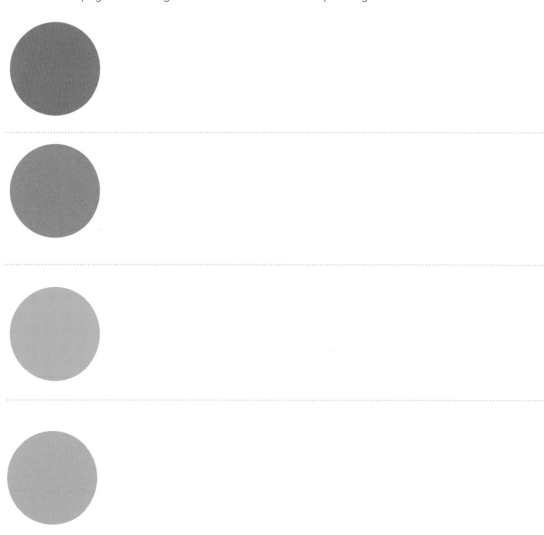

22

Give yourself a natural foot massage. Walk with
bare feet on small stones to massage your soles.

23

Although it may look as if nothing's happening, everything in nature is constantly changing. The grass is growing. Leaves are growing. Seeds are sprouting. It's happening slowly, too slowly for us to see, but it's happening. Find a place in nature to sit for a while. Be still and think of everything that is happening that you're not able to see.

24

Grey day? Go outside! While from the inside it may look like the day is only grey and gloomy, once you're out in nature you'll notice that a grey day can have many beautiful moments: misty, mystical landscapes, sunrays breaking through the clouds, a sudden rainbow. Make notes about what you can see in and beyond the greyness.

25

Collect leaves from a couple of different trees. Try to look at them without labelling them. Hold them up to the sunlight and see the difference in how the sunlight shines through them. Notice their different colours and delicate nerves. Smell the leaves and feel their structure with your fingertips.

26

Every part of the day has its own quality of light. In the morning, as the sun rises, the world gets brighter every minute. In the evening, when the sun sets, the light takes on a softer tone. Take photographs at different times during the day and become aware of the changing nature of light.

27

When you take the time to sit and look, nature reveals its hidden beauty. Sit in the long grass and look for the spider webs that are stretched between the blades of grass, sometimes with drops of dew upon them, sparkling like diamonds in the sun.

28

Go outside. Take a moment to allow yourself to truly experience the nature around you. Notice how it makes you feel.

....

....

....

....

29

There is so much to discover near our own homes. When going to the shops, instead of going straight from A to B, take a little detour through an area you don't know well. Stop somewhere and take a look around. What do you see?

....

....

....

....

30

Everything changes, even when you do nothing at all. That can be a refreshing thought, to know the world turns without you. Sit down in a green area and take a minute to realise that everything around you is slowly growing and changing.

CHAPTER 4

Move Your Body

Whether going for an evening run or consciously stretching the many muscles and ligaments of your feet, your body in motion is a complete marvel. We know that movement makes us feel better — and even the smallest incremental choices all add up to a body that feels and functions well. That's the thing with mindful movement — it doesn't need to be big, bold or exhausting (in fact, we'd suggest that anything that doesn't actually feel good is not worth the effort!), but a gentle morning stretch, tapping your toes to some music or a speedy burst of jumping jacks costs nothing — not even much of your time — but will repay you with both a mood and energy boost. What's not to love? As you work your way through the chapter, feel into the activities that you'd enjoy the most. To make it as easy as possible, we've also focused on incidental movement, which is the sort of 'exercise' you don't even need to plan — you're doing it every time you go up the stairs, vacuum, clean the bathroom or roll around with young kids or a pet — so you're already exercising that habit muscle! We've also included lots of free, easy non-gym ways to get you moving, wherever you are — from simple stretches at home to lengthier practices at the local park. The best way to begin? To just do it! Dive in, explore the possibilities and ask yourself: what one thing can I weave into my day, every day? From the snappiest micro-habits to the longer, more involved practices, each and every one will not only boost your physical health but your mental and emotional health, too.

1

The best movement is incidental — when your body does what it needs to do, naturally and instinctively: cleaning, gardening, parenting. Make a list of five ways in which you intend to move your body today — ways that will leave you feeling energised, not depleted.

1 ....

2 ....

3 ....

4 ....

5 ....

Think about the last time you felt really free and liquid in your body. What were you doing? Jot it down as a 'moving' reminder.

....

....

....

....

....

....

....

....

2

Twenty-eight bones, thirty joints and more than one hundred muscles, tendons and ligaments — that's your feet: biological marvels. But how often do you treat them as such? Squeezed into shoes, hidden beneath socks — it's time to resurrect your soles! The simple act of redistributing your weight can help: fifty per cent on each foot, with fifty per cent between the ball and heel of each foot. If you catch yourself off-kilter, re-align. Keep doing so, until you begin to feel that sense of natural balance.

3

Laughter yoga is a modern form of yoga that involves long periods of voluntary laughter. Shake your body and limbs for five minutes to loosen and warm up. Now begin 'laughing' by repeating 'ho ho ha ha ha' and smiling. Repeat until the urge to laugh comes over you. It's a wonderful antidote to a stressful day. Try it!

4

In summer, when it's been really hot all day, sunset is the nicest time to be active outside. Go for a run or a walk in the evening. See how the trees catch the last sunrays. Enjoy the cooling down of the earth while you take deep breaths.

5

Flamingos are perhaps the most iconic waterbirds. Why do they stand on one leg? Scientists have only recently discovered that it's actually more comfortable for them to stand on one leg instead of two. It costs them less energy. For humans, it's entirely the opposite; to stand on one foot, we need our full attention. That's why one-legged standing poses in yoga make us forget daily worries — we need to concentrate on keeping our balance. Try to stand on one leg, clearing your head and becoming one with your body.

6

Surya Namaskar are the yoga moves to greet the sun, also known as the sun salutation, and nothing beats the feeling of practising it outside. In the Vedic tradition, the sun is symbolic of consciousness. Don't force anything; just accept the state of your body as it is in this moment.

7

Practise meditative walking in an open field.
Walk more quickly than you usually would
and set your gaze just above the horizon.
After a while you will forget it is you who is
walking: the 'self' disappears, and you reach
a state of flow.

8

We are advised to walk at least 10,000 steps a day. Most smartphones
have a standard pedometer, which can measure your daily step count.
Note how many steps you take every day this week. Think of ways to
increase your step count.

Monday

....

Tuesday

....

Wednesday

....

Thursday

....

Friday

....

Saturday

....

Sunday

....

9

Hills are sometimes former mountains that have been worn down by erosion over many thousands of years; sometimes they are human-made. Some rolling landscapes were sculpted by glaciers long ago. Hills may be less impressive than mountains, but they can be beautiful, nonetheless. And they're easy to climb. The fact that we humans like views so much has to do with evolutionary psychology. Being able to see possible danger from a distance makes us feel safe. A broad view also helps our creative thinking. Climb a hill today.

10

Can't stop the constant repetition of negative thoughts? Go for a brisk walk in nature. Research carried out at Stanford University in California, USA, showed that a ninety-minute walk in a green environment deactivates the part in your brain associated with negative thinking. Note your thoughts before and after the walk.

Before	After

11

Walking together is a powerful way to connect with someone. The calming effect of nature, the fact that you're not looking directly at each other but have each other's attention, and the fact that there is less chance of being disrupted, makes people talk more freely. Even if a big part of the walk is in silence, people experience a deep sense of togetherness during a walk. Invite someone to come on a walk with you.

12

Taking a rest outside in nature is one of the best things there is. When you're on a hike, take a break when you feel tired and lie down in a sunny spot. Listen to the sounds, the wind, the peaceful nothing. If possible, take a short nap. Slowly start moving your fingers and feet before you get up again. Start by noticing the sounds, smelling the ground. Mindfully, get up and continue your hike.

13

We do feel better after a workout in a green environment – that's a fact. But sometimes it's hard to get motivated. It's no wonder: we have evolved to save up energy. We have to fight our natural impulse to choose the lazy option. A good tip to help you overcome any resistance is to commit to starting and nothing else. Don't set a big goal; don't overthink it; just start with a two-minute warm-up. Once your blood starts flowing, your reluctance will melt away.

14

Just a short burst of energy can have a significant positive impact on your mood when you are in nature – even doing something as simple as jumping jacks. Stand with your feet together and your arms by your side. Hop and land with your feet apart at the same time as bringing your arms above your head. Then hop again and bring your feet and arms back together again. Repeat this until you feel your heart rate rising and your blood pumping.

15

The philosopher Henry David Thoreau believed that, 'An early morning walk is a blessing for the whole day.' Go out in the early morning for a run or a brisk walk to see the sunrise. The air will still be moist, with dewdrops covering the ground and everything on it. Come home refreshed and ready for the rest of the day.

16

Swimming in open water will make you stronger, mentally and physically. There is some scientific evidence that regular wild swimming can ameliorate mild depression symptoms. Put on a wetsuit and head to the nearest body of natural water where you can swim.

17

In his book *Mindful Thoughts for Cyclists*, Nick Moore says: 'There's nothing wrong with confining your cycling to warm summer days, but for true understanding, we must know cold, not just heat, and embrace the dark as well as the light.' Take a bike ride on a cool, crisp morning and feel the cold, fresh air reinvigorating you.

18

Relax using a simple reclining yoga twist. Lying on your back on the floor, draw both knees in to your chest. Open your arms to the sides, like wings, and let your knees fall gently to one side. Move your head slowly from one side to the other. How does it feel when your head faces the same direction as your knees? And facing the opposite direction? Repeat, with your knees falling to the opposite side, and compare how it feels.

19

If you've seen a dog getting up after a nap, you'll know immediately why there is a yoga asana (position) that is called 'downward-facing dog.' It is generally the first move that a dog makes after waking up. Harvard University researchers say that people should stretch every day to keep their joints flexible. Make it a habit to stretch every time you get up from a resting position — just like a dog.

20

To fight the afternoon slump at work, don't automatically reach for the coffee; instead, stand up and go for a short walk. Brain research has shown that walking stimulates part of the brain that functions as an engine for your mind. This enhances mental arousal, helping you to think more clearly. That's why walking meetings can be far more inspiring and productive than trying to force concentration in a brightly lit meeting room. Make notes of when you can arrange a walking meeting instead of a sitting one.

21

Who needs the gym if you have a park? You can create your own exercise routine around your garden or park. Jump over logs, stretch against a tree — you can even make running more interesting by avoiding things on the ground, such as twigs or leaves. That way you're not only training your body but also your cognitive capacities. Design an exercise plan that works in your outside space and draw the different activities here.

22

Qigong and tai chi are ways to guide your energy (chi) as it moves through and around your body. They can help many people to find inner peace and strength. When performed outside in nature, these activities can be extra special. Here's a simple qigong exercise: with your arms by your side, raise your hands from your hips to chest height with palms facing up while breathing in; return them, with palms facing down, while breathing out. Feel the difference when moving your arms up and down.

23

Do you know all the green areas in your town or city? Are there public gardens you might not know of? Check a map and go out and explore the areas of green on a run or a brisk walk. Note where you've found a green space in your area, however small.

24

Sport is about more than staying fit; if you're not having fun while exercising, you've chosen the wrong kind of sport. Maybe playing badminton on the street with a neighbour is more your thing, or dancing in your living room, or biking in nature. Write down three sport activities that you think you'd enjoy or which have already brought you joy in the past. Pick one to do this week.

1 ....
....

2 ....
....

3 ....
....

25

Walking the stairs is free exercise! Be aware of all the stairs that you replace with lifts and other moving devices.

26

Pull up your shoulders and drop them again. Repeat three times. Notice the difference before and after.

27

A great way to create body awareness is with dance isolations. Put on some upbeat music and sit down on a bench. First only tap your feet to the beat. After that, just move your shoulders. Then do the same with your hips, head, etc. Try to stay in the moment, let go of all thoughts and notice what happens in your body.

28

A fine way to wander without a goal is to go on a 'heart-walk', where you let yourself be guided by symbols. Whenever you see a heart shape (or another interesting shape) in a tree, or in a puddle, go that way.

29

'All truly great thoughts are conceived while walking,'
said the philosopher Friedrich Nietzsche. He was right.
Modern brain research shows that walking has a
positive effect on cognitive processes and can literally
lead to more 'wisdom'. Go for a walk and write down
your thoughts afterwards.

....

....

....

....

....

....

....

30

Lie down for a meditative body scan. With every breath, concentrate on a
different part of your body, starting at your toes and ending with the top of
your head. Try to relax every muscle along the way. Perform a second body
scan at a different time and, again, note where you found it hard to let
tension go. Did you notice a difference?

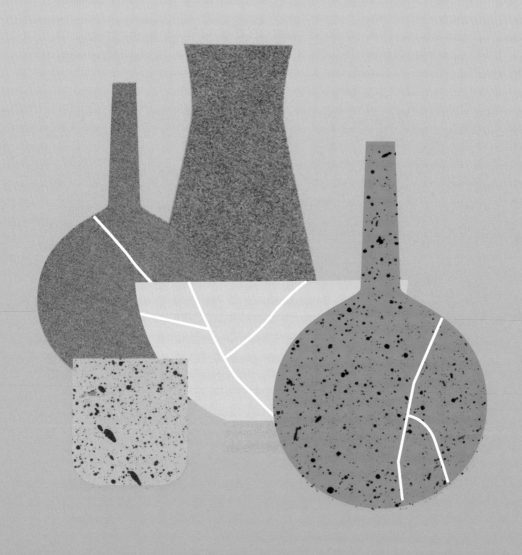

CHAPTER 5

Declutter & Clarify

The promise of a clean, uncluttered home is a very appealing one, but many of us are consuming more than ever before (we now own twice as many possessions as those who lived fifty years ago) even while our desire to live a minimalistic life is at a record high. Clearly, there's a disconnect here! In this creative, fun-loving chapter, the aim is simple — and it begins by feeling into the reasons you want to live in a clean and uncluttered environment in the first place. Once you're clear on that, we've also suggested lots of nourishing ways to turn your home space into an eco, soothing, streamlined place to hang out. There may be a few big ideas that really pique your interest (this is the 'cue' and 'craving' part of our habit formation cycle), so you could also try breaking bigger goals into micro-steps that you complete over a series of days... knowing, too, that each and every time you return to your goal, you're also helping a new habit to stick. Remember, too, that our desire to declutter can also impact our environment — so please do ensure that you remove anything responsibly — by donating, selling, gifting or disposing with due diligence (your local council will have information on how to do this, particularly if you're removing electrical appliances or old furniture). You could also look into the many free 'marketplaces' online, where locals can express interest and then scoop items off your hands — leaving you with more time to enjoy your newly decluttered space, and focus on the habits you want to embed to keep your home clear, calm and a pleasure to live in.

1

The dynamics of our daily spaces have a huge impact on our sense of wellbeing. Too much clutter, not enough light, doors that don't fully open, lack of fresh air or greenery – all can impede our ability to create joy. Read on to take a space survey.

Which room do you spend the most time in? On a scale of 1 to 5, think about how you feel in the space: 1 is least joyful, 5 is most.

....

....

....

....

....

Let your heart guide you around the room. What areas feel problematic, dingy, unloved? Note them down here.

....

....

....

....

....

2

Look around you: does your space need an update? Does clutter need to be cleared? Does more light need to be invited in? Do you need a bit more greenery? A lick of paint? Shake up your everyday space. Draw a plan of your main living space then have fun thinking about how you could rearrange it, maybe with a cosy corner for your favourite reading chair.

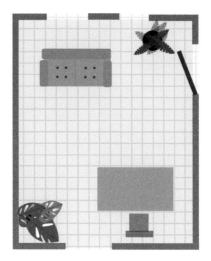

3

For many of us, our working space is also where we spend the most time. Ensure your working environment is conducive to joy: select flowers or plants, place pictures or artwork, scent the room with candles or a diffuser. Once you've invited joy into the space, how does the way you approach work change?

4

Open any drawer in your house. Take everything out. Count the number of items. In the drawer opposite draw only the things you really need, then place these real items back in the drawer.

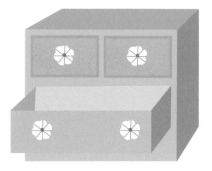

5

Move from room to room, letting your eyes fall on things you are not wholly fond of. If it doesn't 'spark joy' (a term coined by minimalist Marie Kondo), set it aside.

6

Today, it's easier than ever to do your bit for the environment. Why not start at home? Most household cleaning jobs need only one of three inexpensive things – vinegar, sodium bicarbonate or soap (pure liquid Castile soap is a great natural option). Fill these bottles-for-life with your chosen cleaning combos and then make them for yourself.

What does what?

Vinegar = Descales; great for making glass shine when mixed 50/50 with water.

Sodium bicarbonate = Absorbs odour; great in an open jar in the fridge or sprinkled over a carpet before vacuuming.

Vinegar + sodium bicarbonate = Great for unblocking pipes, cleaning ovens, scouring sinks and floors.

Vinegar + Castile soap = An amazing all-natural, all-purpose cleaning solution.

Make your bottle-for-life combinations more fragrant with a few drops of essential oil. The following are also naturally antibacterial: lemon, tea tree, sage, rosemary, eucalyptus, cedarwood and peppermint.

7

The average person owns twice as many things as someone who lived fifty years ago. Back then, many people had to rely on resourcefulness and ingenuity to make do with what they had rather than finding cheap, quick-fix solutions. Have fun giving each of these everyday objects a new lease of life. While you work, think about how many different ways each can be used.

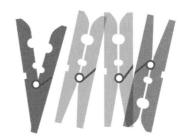

8

Many of us are now saying no to single-use plastic. But, inevitably, we all have some old plastic bottles hanging around at home. Resist the urge to throw them away; find a new use for them instead. Make a bird feeder from an old bottle. Cut a small window in the side of the bottle so that the birds can land on it to feed. Don't make it so large that seeds pour out. Make some small holes in the bottom of the bottle so that any rainwater can drain. Hang the feeder from a branch using a piece of wire or string secured around the fastened bottle cap.

9

Take a peek inside your recycling bin. What items are most commonly found there? Think about which of them you can source in a different, wastefree way, to keep the bin as empty as possible next time.

10

Let's take a look inside the wardrobe. Count the number of clothes you have in there. Now, write down the number of clothes you have worn in the past six months. And the number you have not. If you own clothes you love, but never seem to wear, move them to the front of your wardrobe and look forward to wearing them this week.

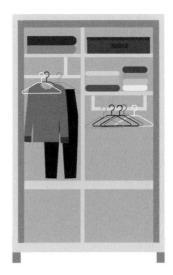

11

Set aside a morning to line up all the clothing and accessories that you love, but which are in need of repair. Save up the money you need to take them to a good tailor, seamstress or cobbler, and have them renewed for life.

12

Take a photograph of an item in your house that no longer 'sparks joy' and send it to someone you think might like to offer it a new home. Or, upload the picture to a community sales platform, and see if it interests someone else.

13

Oiling wooden tools, boards and furniture to protect them from damage leaves them gleaming and is a wonderfully meditative activity. Work in soothing, circular motions... just like the inner rings of a tree.

14

Think about your most disposable household items, and how you can replace them with something of beauty, personal value and meaning, with a view to reclaiming joy in the process. For example, make bright, beautiful and reusable cleansing cloths from scraps of pretty fabric or resurrect the handkerchief to replace facial tissues. Embroider your name or a cheery picture in the corner.

15

Fast fashion has created a world in which items of clothing are as cheap as they are throwaway, and the environmental impact is enormous. We rarely save up for something that we really want. What single item of clothing do you really need or want that you would be willing to save up for? Treat yourself to it only when you can afford it. How does it feel?

16

Set yourself a goal of refusing to buy any new clothing for a month. Then another... and keep going. If you need to replace something, consider seeking out a secondhand alternative first. After all, there's joy-a-plenty waiting to be reclaimed in secondhand and charity shops.

17

The best advice regarding mindful consumerism is to wait a full week before buying something you want. If the 'want' dulls in that time, it is not worth it. Use this shopper to store scribbles of the few things you currently want, but won't buy until at least a week has passed.

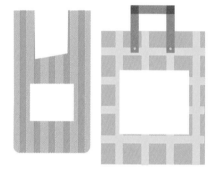

18

Most unloved items simply need a good clean for a new lease of life — think of the vibrant light that floods in when you clean your windows. Imagine what's on the other side of these just-washed windowpanes.

19

Unmendable and faded textiles have many uses. If you've a pile of clothes that are too shabby to sell or donate, cut them up to use as cleaning cloths and surface wipes, saving the less-shabby parts for craft projects.

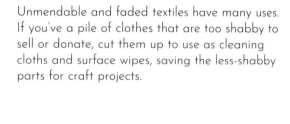

20

Studies have shown that we gain almost as much joy from window shopping and browsing as we do from physically purchasing things. If you're consumed by the consumer itch, try doing this for a week. You may be surprised to find that your urges are curbed.

21

If you could learn one new skill to help you make and mend more effectively at home, what would it be? Write it down here, along with the first step you'll take today.

22

It's natural to feel in colour. A relaxing room may feel 'greenish-blue', while a bright, sunny room feels 'orange'. Enjoy creating a colour code for the rooms in your home. Revisit it next season. Has it changed?

23

Transform the humble tub into a place of peace and joy. Add flower petals, scented oil, salt, herbs, clays and even crystals to the water to elevate an everyday soak into a restorative ritual. Here is some joyful bath inspiration:

Rose petals + magnesium salt = deeply relaxing

Oats + calendula = skin-soothing

Rosemary + Epsom salts = invigorating

24

Essential oils bring joy-boosting benefits to all manner of daily duties. Proven mood-lifters include rose, lemon, neroli, tangerine and basil. Why not add a drop or two of joyful essential oils to a piece of paper, let it dry, and then slide it into this book? Each time you open it, you'll have a scented smile awaiting you.

25

The trend for tiny homes shows that more people are valuing their quality of life over the size of their abodes. When space is so limited, you're forced to choose only what you need and love. Whenever you consider what to bring into your home, give it the 'tiny home treatment'. Ask yourself: do I need it? Do I love it? A 'no', means 'no'.

26

All homes are made lovelier and healthier with the addition of some well-chosen houseplants. These air-purifying plants are ideal for city living, being as hardy as they are hardworking. Fill your house with plants! A NASA study found that houseplants were able to remove ninety per cent of the chemicals that were blown into a test room. The plants found to be best at cleaning the air were the Barberton (gerbera) daisy, English ivy and the snake plant (mother-in-law's tongue). Monsteras may be less effective, but they grow bigger.

27

Found objects can make for wonderful wall hangings. From dried and pressed flowers housed in a simple frame, to a piece of driftwood that can be mounted to make a simple shelf, challenge yourself to see utility and beauty in the used and the ordinary.

28

Every home has its own unique scent. You are aware of it the moment you walk in, be it wet dog or freshly baked bread. What would your 'uniquely you' home smell like? Lavender and rosemary keep their scent long after they're dried. Dry fresh herbs by hanging them upside down tied with string. You can also keep them in a pocket made of cheesecloth or muslin in your closet or under your pillow. A house that smells of natural herbs is not only pleasant but also calming for the mind.

29

Taking care of plants will help to take your mind off daily worries and reduce tension. When watering plants, make it a mindful activity. Hear the water soaking into the soil; picture the plant's roots drinking it up; smell the fresh, green fragrance released.

30

Every time you come home, greet your space as you would a fond, old friend. Come up with a greeting and enjoy saying it out loud (or thinking it, if you have company), to mark your joyful crossing over the threshold. Write your greeting here.

CHAPTER 6

Nourish & Hydrate

Food is life — not only the fuel that powers us to do what we choose to do, but also a daily form of nourishment, enrobed in joy and pleasure! But sometimes it's easy to get stuck in a food rut — buying and eating the same things over and over, without really considering what it is you actually crave, or what would really nourish you. To help you on this journey, we've focused on the many ways in which you can invite more nutritious goodness into your life, while also considering what may grow season by season, what can be found in your local area, and where other things you enjoy actually come from. Because once we start thinking about all the ways in which we can look after ourselves and the world around us through food, we begin to build happy little pathways in our brains that transform our relationship with what's on our plate — making every meal an opportunity for enjoyment, nourishment and gratitude. From the first summer strawberry to the last autumn pear, food really is worth celebrating — and not only the food we pick up at our local supermarkets, but the stuff we'd ordinarily discard, or walk straight past without a second look. To that end, we've filled this yummy chapter with practical foraging and frugal tips, alongside delicious herbal recipes and childhood meal memories — all designed to whet your appetite! And even as you curl up with (the inarguable comfort of) a cosy cuppa, we hope you have fun working through these nourishing suggestions — learning new skills, feeling inspired and perhaps even looking at the food on your plate in a more playful (or grateful) way, too.

1

Which part of your body needs nourishment today? Scan from the top of your head to the tips of your toes and see where your attention goes. Write down what you feel when you focus on each area.

2

Eating with full concentration can transform every bite — from the smell, colour and texture of the food, to the way its flavour alters depending on what part of the tongue it touches. Start small — try a berry or a chocolate button — and give it your full attention while you eat it. Does it taste different?

3

We tend to think about food in terms of nutritional value, rather than the qualities, textures and aromas it possesses. Enjoy a meal by thinking about why it is good — is it sweet, sour, salty, pungent, bitter, astringent? Is it dry and rough, or smooth and silky? Bringing awareness to your food heightens your appreciation and joy, too.

4

What do you crave right now? Add it to your shopping list.

5

Do you have a favourite recipe that a friend or family member cooks for you, but you cannot make yourself? Ask them to share the recipe with you. Make it when you need reminding of the special bond you share.

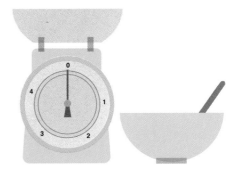

6

Snip nourishing and delicious recipes out of magazines and decide on one evening a week when you will actually enjoy them.

7

Soup: it's great! You can put everything in it and you just have to stir. You can invite everyone last minute because you can easily make more. It's comforting, it's hot, it's easy to eat and it's full of nutrition. Describe your favourite soup.

8

Natural foods give off their scent when they are ripe — the natural sugars are at their peak, bringing sweetness to the food's flavour and aroma. Smell an unripe piece of fruit. Smell it again when it is ripe. Does anything happen to your tongue or mouth as you smell?

9

When we eat leafy vegetables, we are literally tasting the colour green. A large part of the flavour is from chlorophyll, which the plants use to capture sunlight for photosynthesis and which makes them green. So, if you eat a green leafy vegetable, it's nice to think that you're eating sunlight.

10

What produce does this season offer you? Sometimes eating seasonal fruit and vegetables is just what you need. When you live in a country with cold winters, for example, and you eat kale, a winter vegetable, your body gets the iron that it needs. Find out what fruit and vegetables are seasonal right now and prepare a meal or snack with some of them.

11

Thinking about the qualities and tastes of your favourite foods, consider how your cravings change through the year. This is nature's way of nourishing you — making you crave precisely what is most fresh and 'in season'. Spend a few minutes imagining the tastes of each season: fresh, crunchy and green in spring; water-rich, light and juicy in summer; sweet, earthy and warming in autumn; rich and hearty in winter.

12

Eating is a great opportunity to practise mindfulness. We stop what we're doing to satisfy our hunger and at the same time we can connect to our senses. When eating, take time to notice the different flavours in each mouthful. Close your eyes as you chew to focus on the taste.

13

Go to the supermarket and look for something you've never eaten before, something exotic. This is even more fun if you're in another country. Take it home and try it. Describe and draw it here.

What is it? ....

Taste? ....

Origin? ....

14

The journeys taken by ingredients to reach our cooking pots are often mindblowing adventures, so be mindful of where your food comes from. Choose one thing you ate today and try to answer these questions:

Where did it come from or grow?	Who was in contact with it before you?
How did it get to your town or area?	How did it get to your kitchen?

15

We are so used to buying our food from shops that we sometimes forget the ways people used to collect food themselves. We still could; there are so many wildflowers and weeds that we can eat. The young leaves of a dandelion; the flowers of a purple violet; the flowers of the nasturtium; the leaves of ground elders. Investigate the edible weeds and flowers that grow in your neighbourhood and make a flower salad. Double-check online that what you find is edible. Make sure that nothing you pick is chemically treated or found next to a busy road.

16

For our ancestors, the forest was one big salad bar. In springtime or early summer, you can make a forest salad with the buds and young leaves of beech; autumn, you can eat its nuts. Never eat anything if you don't know what it is in case it is poisonous. Make notes and drawings of edible forest plants.

17

These ten commonly wasted veggie and fruit scraps are as useful as they are tasty. By adding unfamiliar and frugal flourishes to your everyday food, you up the nutritional benefits as well as the deliciousness quotient.

Apple Skin is high in natural pectin, making it ideal for jam-making.

Orange Peel can be candied and added to baked goods.

Fennel fronds make the most delicious fresh tea.

Herby Stalks such as parsley and coriander are great in soups and stocks.

Carrot Tops have a grassy, sweet flavour; they are brilliant whizzed up with garlic and basil to make pesto.

Celery Leaves are sweet and tender; they're delicious in juices, salads, soups and stocks.

Beetroot Leaves are similar to Swiss chard; wilt with butter or olive oil and a pinch of sea salt.

Stir-fry **Broccoli Stalks** with garlic, ginger, soy sauce and sesame oil.

Leek and **Spring Onion** cuttings add brilliant flavour to stock.

Pair **Potato Peelings** with rapeseed oil and sea salt, and roast in the oven for crispy skins that you can top or dip.

18

Keep a cotton bag in your freezer and add your scraps to it whenever you're preparing veg. The next time you make stock for soup, simply tip the contents into the pot, saving time, effort and money.

19

A ripe red tomato is one of summer's sweetest delights. If you have grown or bought more than you need, don't let a bite go to waste. Simply whiz up with a pinch of sea salt and some fresh basil or oregano, for perfect passata that can be frozen for up to six months.

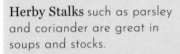

20

Tea tastes so much nicer when made with fresh, rather than dried, herbs and flowers. Pop seasonal herbs into these four steaming mugs. Use the seasonal suggestions here or add your own.

Spring: Nettles, fennel, dandelion, lemon balm

Summer: Lavender, rose, lemon verbena, chamomile

Autumn: Thyme, mint, sage

Winter: Rosehip, ginger, rosemary

21

Herbs have long been an integral part of taking care of ourselves. For every little pain, our ancestors knew a natural remedy. On this page are herbs that can reduce anxiety. Pour hot water over their fresh or dried leaves and flowers. Savour the aroma and drink the infusion with a mindful presence. 'Only in the awareness of the present, can your hands feel the pleasant warmth of the cup,' according to Thich Nhat Hanh, Zen Buddhist monk.

Jasmine (*Jasminum*)

Valerian (*Valeriana officinalis*)

Sweet basil (*Ocimum basilicum*)

Bergamot (*Citrus bergamia*)

Fennel (*Foeniculum vulgare*)

Chamomile (*Matricaria chamomilla*)

Marjoram (*Origanum majorana*)

22

One way to gently extract a herb's healing power is to make sun tea — for example, try using chamomile. Clean a bunch of chamomile flowers and add them to a jar of cold water. Let it stand in the sun for several hours, then remove the flowers. Sweeten the resulting infusion with some honey. Let it cool down, then add ice cubes, a slice of lemon, some mint leaves and fresh chamomile flowers.

23

Ginger is one of the best spices to give you a boost on a cold day. Place 2 cm (¾ inch) sliced and peeled ginger root in a mug of boiling water. Add honey and some fresh lemon juice. Let it brew for five to ten minutes and then enjoy the warming infusion.

24

A jug of water can be an opportunity for joy. Source a pleasing secondhand vessel and, after a good clean, fill it with filtered water, fresh herbs, berries or slices of lime or lemon. Sip away while you work. Transform a daily 'must' into a welcome pleasure.

25

Thinking back to our childhood is a great way to remind us of our true passions and unearth the playful selves who can get lost under layers of adulthood and responsibility. What was your favourite meal when you were a child? Write down one memory of having that meal.

26

Special treats can link to happy childhood memories. Think of a sweet treat that made you happy as a child. Draw it and tap into your memory by describing it.

27

Make a wild, eccentrically decorated cake. Put all your favourite sweet ingredients on it. Make it as crazy as you can. Invite your friends and neighbours to help you eat it.

28

When we feel bad about something, drinking a hot beverage immediately lifts our spirits a little bit. Researchers found that drinking something warm even makes a person friendlier. Get the kettle on and draw your tea or coffee cup.

29

Lunch is so often squeezed into our busy schedules that some people no longer even sit down for it, taking a sandwich or a bagel on the run while doing a hundred other things at once. Not today! Describe your favourite lunch and make the description as mouth-watering and enticing as possible. Then treat yourself by bringing it to life.

....

....

....

....

30

Eat something with an awareness of what it does for your body and make notes about your experience. Is it refreshing? Does it give you energy, fill you up or feel as if it's giving you a nutritional boost?

CHAPTER 7

Hope & Gratitude

It's hard to believe that something as simple as counting your blessings can have such a transformative effect on your life — but countless studies over the last ten years, in the fields of positive psychology and behavioural science, have revealed just how powerful this humble, daily practice can be. Throughout this feel-good chapter, we explore the many ways in which we can give thanks for the extraordinary within the ordinary — from the people in our lives we're most grateful for to the memories that remind us of what matters most. We also take a deep dive into the micro-steps that build up to form long-term happiness habits — from adding supportive sayings to your phone or computer (which pop up at regular intervals) to repeated thanks-giving goals that help exercise that gratitude muscle. You can choose to simply draw your mind to the good stuff in the present moment, or you can take time at the top or tail end of each day, to jot things down. Likewise, you can calendarise happy reminders, leave notes for yourself around the home or have fun printing off copies of photos you've not looked at in years... whatever feels like the most natural way for you to tune into the things in your own life that you are truly thankful for. And because studies have also shown that the less we focus on the negatives and the more we wire our minds towards the stuff we're grateful for — building new neural pathways towards positivity — the better we'll also become at spotting the silver linings in the most challenging situations. It can even help us operate from an auto-optimistic mindset in the future, too. Now, isn't that something to feel truly grateful for?

1

Write down joyous memories for whenever you need a reminder of your blessings.

2

With so much of our communication reliant on our devices, we've lost the joy of curling up with a stack of old letters and reminiscing. Find a favourite message on your phone and write it out here to keep forever.

3

Did you know that even if your smile is fake, your brain registers it as a positive response and that can lift the mood? Choose a day to set yourself reminders to smile more (even when you may not feel like it). You may be surprised at how much better you feel at the day's end.

4

When we keep special notes, letters and sketches in drawers or folders, we miss out on the joy of seeing them all the time. Invest in a beautiful large picture or poster frame, or elegant pinboard, and make a point of curating, displaying and enjoying your life's precious paper memories.

5

Who has been a good friend to you in this lifetime? To whom have you been a good friend? Remember to reach out, not only to value and thank your friends for all they do for you, but for what you do, too — for others and for yourself.

6

When did you last laugh until you cried? Colour in these happy tears.

7

Imagine your heart is its own joy box and that each time something kind, positive or hopeful happens, a little more joy feeds into the space in your chest. One of the best ways to grow this inner glow is by practising gratitude. Don't let good things go unacknowledged – WITNESS them, FEEL them, GIVE THANKS for them.

8

What was the last bit of good news you received that made you want to skip around the room? Close your eyes and let the memory of it fill you up.

9

If you have family members or friends who knew you well as a child, give them a call and ask them to share the funniest memory they have of you as a kid. Remind yourself of this whenever life feels too serious.

10

Make a promise to yourself that you will not save your favourite things 'for best'. Ask yourself, 'Am I not good enough to enjoy my best things, every day?' Every day is a special occasion – you are alive! That's worth celebrating!

11

What makes your heart sing? Fill this heart up to the brim with things you love.

12

Nature can move us deeply — its endless cycles of birth and decay, its beauty and ferocity, its simplicity and complexities. Think of something that fascinates you about nature. What is the first thing that comes to mind?

13

Write a letter to yourself as you are now, from the perspective of yourself as a young child. What advice would you offer? What hopes would you share?

14

A sunset will never lose the power to give people a feeling of awe: the grandness of it, the magical colours, the connection with time passing and days ending. Think of moments when you've witnessed a beautiful sunset.

15

A lot of plants use other plants as support to grow, because they lack a sturdy stem. Sometimes they help the host plant by sharing glucose. Sometimes a plant suffocates its host. Just like human relations, these relationships can be supportive or stifling. Think about the people close to you. Who gives you energy and who can be a bit draining?

16

The petals of a flower turn towards the sun to catch its rays. In a field of sunflowers, it's hard to miss the fact that the flower heads turn to face the sun. Stop and reflect on your own movement towards things that energise and strengthen you. Do you turn towards them as much as you'd like to?

17

Look at the natural wonders checklist below.
Which would you like to visit? What natural sights
have you already seen that blew your socks off?
Add your own natural wonders to the list.

A giant sequoia tree

A roaring waterfall

A glacier bathed in morning light

A cherry blossom park in springtime

A rain forest in the mist

A desert sunset

The northern lights (aurora borealis)

Heather fields in the evening sun

A towering cliff

18

Forget about skydiving! Make a bucket list of tiny daily pleasures. Keep your wishes as small — and achievable — as possible. What would you like to do or experience more of?

19

Fewer than half of us print photographs anymore. Tip this trend by spending a quiet hour selecting a handful of special images on your phone. Print them out and display them in a frame, the good old-fashioned way.

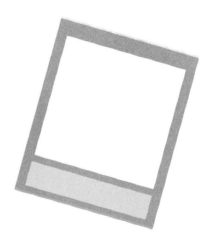

20

There is always something to appreciate about your ordinary day, even if your routine seems monotonous and you live for the weekend — you just have to look for it! Make two quick sketches of what you like about a typical day.

21

Draw your favourite person from your neighbourhood.

22

What do you feel most thankful for in this very moment?

....

....

....

....

23

There are probably many people you don't really know who form part of your daily routine and you form part of theirs. With yourself in the middle of this space, draw the people with whom you share your existence: work colleagues, your kids' friends, your yoga teacher, even people you see in the bus queue.

Me

24

Focus only on positive things today. Jot down or draw five positive things right now. Notice how focusing on the positive affects your mood.

1 ....

2 ....

3 ....

4 ....

5 ....

25

The media tends to focus on negative news. Check today's newspaper and look for something positive that happened.

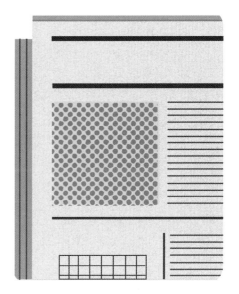

26

Noticing everything you have to be thankful for can boost your wellbeing and even improve your health and sleep. But it can be difficult to stay in that mindset and remember the importance of gratitude. It helps if you give it a place in your evening routine. Try noting three things you are grateful for every day for the next week.

Day 1: Today I am grateful for

Day 2: Today I am grateful for

Day 3: Today I am grateful for

Day 4: Today I am grateful for

Day 5: Today I am grateful for

Day 6: Today I am grateful for

Day 7: Today I am grateful for

27

Research shows that supportive friends are extremely important to your wellbeing. Think about how your friends support you. Which friend comes to mind first? Write about them, and how they've supported you.

....

....

....

....

....

....

....

....

28

Connect with your feet. Your feet take you everywhere; they're working all day long. Give them a nice massage and take a moment to be aware of them and thankful for the amazing job that they do.

29

Positive emotions open you up 'like a flower opening up to the sun,' says the American researcher Barbara Fredrickson. So, it helps to think of the good things in your life if you want to embark on a creative task. Write down all that's positive in your life now.

30

Remind yourself regularly of mantras and sayings that inspire and uplift you. Add them at intervals to your phone's calendar. Each time one pops up with a happy alert, it'll be like receiving mail from a great friend. Make a list of your favourites here to get you started.

CHAPTER 8

Joy & Kindness

Flowing on from our growing gratitude habit in Chapter Seven, comes the crucial practice of kindness. Where would we be without a hand to hold, a shoulder to cry on or a smile to support us? Kindness is the glue that sticks us together... that allows us to overcome the bleakest days and toughest challenges. And if you spend just a few seconds thinking about an act of kindness bestowed upon you, you'll probably feel something shift in your chest... a spreading warmth, possibly followed by a smile. The real magic comes in realising that YOU have that power, too — the power to make someone else smile, or give something a second chance, or feel more hopeful about the day ahead. So, in this warm hug of a chapter we explore the many ways in which you can both give and receive kindness — from putting the past's wrongs to right, to inscribing your very own graduation from 'the school of your life' with your greatest gifts and qualities (because we all need a regular pat on the back). We also explore the ways in which we can be more mindful of our words and actions — creating kinder habits that might save us future heartache, or leave a trail of loveliness in our wake. And because modern life often rushes on without a moment's breath, there are plenty of 'pause' moments, too — reminding us that we deserve to stop and smell the roses, connect with the beautiful world around us, and even find moments of kinship with our four-legged friends. Whatever you find yourself meditating on in this chapter, embrace your kindness instinct with a whole heart... it'll do you (and those in your life) nothing but the world of good.

1

List one thing that you will do tomorrow, to promote joy in another.

....

....

....

....

....

2

Draw your wondrous reflection in this mirror or add a photo of yourself
into this space, if you prefer. What loving words and thoughts will you have
each and every day? Write them down in thought bubbles.

....

....

....

....

....

....

....

....

3

What's the loveliest thing anyone has ever said to you? If you have already forgotten, it's time to begin writing them down. Save this space for the expressions of love and joy that people share with you. Read back on these whenever you need an emotional boost.

4

Add a joyful gesture to a day in your diary, as a treat to enjoy later in the week.

5

Write a love letter to yourself as though you are your own best friend.
Thank yourself for all that you have done over the years – the laughter,
the adventures, the learning curves and kindnesses. Pop your letter into the
envelope, and send it back to yourself when you are ready to receive it.

6

Be the reason someone smiles today. When you think a kind thought, don't
keep it to yourself. Share it with the person who made you think it and watch
that kindness multiply.

7

Annotate these lovely kindness notes with 'pats on the back' for all you have to be proud of. Stick them where you'll see them each day: at your desk, on the bathroom mirror, in your purse.

8

Some people beam kindness and happiness from their faces. Have you met someone like that? What do you imagine them thinking, which makes them so? Using the space below, fill this head with happy thoughts.

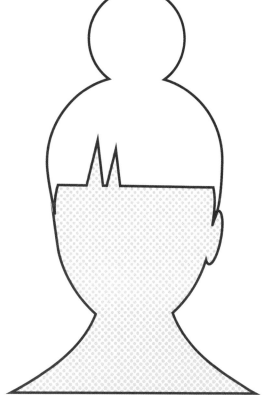

9

Imagine finding an old school report filled with glowing praise of you as a child. Write in all that you wish you had heard back then, here, now.

10

How do you respond when complimented? Do you bat it away, make light of it or simply fail to really believe it? Spend time practising how you will respond to a compliment next time – with grace, gratitude and self-belief.

11

Imagine that you are about to graduate from the school of your life. What qualifications have you earned along your life's path – from resilience to humour, resourcefulness to kindness? Add them to your graduation certificate.

12

It is a sad truth that unkind comments tend to linger longer than kind ones. Make a point of writing down any unkind comments you wish to forget here, in pencil. Now erase them all and write over them with kind comments.

13

Today, try the simple act of counting to ten before allowing an unkind or critical word to leave your lips. Then return to this entry at the day's end. How did it go?

14

Think of the heartache you might save yourself if you just pause for a moment before speaking. Take time to rewrite the script of a conversation you'd like to have again. Then, make peace with what was, and what is, and let it go.

15

If someone acts unfairly, challenge yourself to see that person through an empathetic lens. If their behaviour seems irrational, put yourself in their shoes — what might have made you do the same thing?

16

Compassion is an important part of being mindful. Anger and irritation all get in the way of feeling good. Realising that even the most annoying people in your life have good qualities makes a big difference to how you feel about them. Pick one person you have issues with. Use this space to write about their best traits or to find the positive side to their annoying habits.

Positive   Negative

....

....

....

....

....

....

17

Let's exercise our 'beginner's mind'. Reflect on a time when you went into a situation with a completely open mind. What was the outcome? Now, reflect on a time when you went into a situation with a closed mindset, full of assumptions. What was this outcome?

....

....

....

....

18

Maya Angelou once said: '... people will forget what you said, people will forget what you did, but people will never forget how you made them feel.' How can you choose to live your life today, in ways that will leave a trail of kindess in your wake?

19

A lot of animals live in the city — more than you think. They're sometimes seen as a nuisance, but with humans taking up more and more space, they have had to adapt. Helping urban wildlife will lift your spirits and help you reconnect with nature. You could do the following:

In dry spells, place shallow bowls of water on the ground for bees and small animals.

Help toads and frogs cross roads during the mating season by signing up as a patroller.

Make a peanut string for birds in winter.

Make animal passages in garden fences. Get rid of concrete paving and plant flowers.

20

When we pet a friendly animal, our blood pressure goes down. And when dogs and humans gaze into each other's eyes, something else remarkable happens. Researchers have found that mutual gazing increases levels of oxytocin — a hormone associated with feelings of love and tenderness — in both parties. Write about what you feel when interacting with a house pet.

21

Trees can live to be hundreds of years old. Most trees were here long before us and will outlive us by many years. Many nature religions worship trees as if they are the abodes of spirits. All over the world, people have developed worshipping rituals for trees. Think of an old tree you have a soft spot for, maybe because it's been there all your life or perhaps because it has given you shelter from the sun or rain on occasions. Draw it here. Think of your own little ritual to thank it, maybe by decorating it with flowers or a garland for a day, or by writing a poem about it.

22

'The earth laughs in flowers,' said the American philosopher Ralph Waldo Emerson. Did you know that flowers have the power to make you feel better? Research carried out by the American Society for Horticultural Science found that patients surrounded by flowers needed fewer painkillers and were in a more positive mood than those in rooms with no plants. They also had lower blood pressure and were less anxious and tired. Go out and buy yourself a small bouquet of flowers, because they are worth every penny.

23

A compliment doesn't have to come from your boss, partner or friends to put a smile on your face and keep the positivity circulating. Write yourself a compliment (or two — or three!). You deserve it.

24

Write a letter to your body. When did it help you? When did it hold you back? What are you grateful for? What would you say to it if it could understand you? Be kind and pretend that you're talking to a good friend.

25

We share the planet with millions of other humans, each with their own lives and thoughts, and yet we walk past tens or even hundreds of them each day, making absolutely no connection. Make today the day you smile at everyone you see and don't stop until you get a smile back.

26

Love is all around us! Look for small gestures of affection between other people. Keep an eye out for couples holding hands, parents cuddling their children, friends hugging. Sketch a sweet scene that you saw today.

27

Ask a friend or family member to draw you and point out the things that they love about you.

28

We tend to forget compliments and focus on critique; it's just how humans are wired. It's calculated by researcher John Gottman that in a relationship, nothing fewer than five positive interactions are needed to turn the mad mojo around from one negative interaction. So, focus on the positive today. Note all the compliments that you receive, from anyone, no matter how small, no matter if it's just a look of appreciation or a hand on your shoulder. List them here.

1 ....

2 ....

3 ....

4 ....

5 ....

29

'Metta' means loving kindness, friendliness, amity; it's one of the sublime states of being in Buddhism. A metta-meditation is a compassion meditation where we open our heart to others, but also to ourselves. Jot down some kind thoughts about yourself below. Meditate for five minutes on these thoughts.

....

....

....

....

....

....

30

When you make somebody happy, you become happier yourself; in psychology, that's called 'empathic joy'. Try to tick as many of these boxes with random acts of kindness. In addition to making someone else's day, it might just make you smile.

Let someone go ahead in a queue ☐

Help someone with their food shopping ☐

Smile at a stranger ☐

Offer directions to a person who looks lost ☐

Offer to give someone a lift ☐

Pick up something a kid dropped ☐

Give a heartfelt compliment ☐

CHAPTER 9

Slow & Breathe

'This is me, breathing.' Four words that have the ability to slow us down and bring us back into our bodies. Four words that move us out of shallow, upper-chest autopilot breathing into conscious, deep, restorative breath – a place where the mind slows down, the nervous system regulates and you realise you're not living up here in the mind, but down here, grounded, in your own body. And it's this simple act that forms the foundation of this chapter, which homes in on our one true home – our body – and how to bring it into balance simply by slowing down enough to really be in the present moment. Modern life may rush and race, but we have miniature passports to the present moment scattered all around us – a spot of cloud-watching – and in this chapter we explore the many ways we can build healthy daily habits that keep us from overspending our energy, and help us slow down enough to really live the life we lead. Through nature, through our own senses, and through our interaction between the two, we can unlock so much peaceful potential. And while entire days for rest and reflection may not be possible, choosing to prioritise your 'pause' – whether building in little 'present moment pitstops' while en-route to work or using scent to tap us back into a powerful memory – continually exercises that habit-forming muscle, too. The more you slow down, breathe and notice, the more you'll want to... and though your days won't actually be any less busy, the way you navigate them – with slow and steady rhythm and pockets of breathing space – may just begin to feel like a breath of fresh air...

1

When you breathe in you activate your sympathetic nervous system. When you breathe out you activate your parasympathetic nervous system. The latter stimulates the vagus nerve, which soothes and relaxes you. So, the next time you feel stressed, focus on making your exhale longer than your inhale. The ideal balance is two-to-one. Try it. With each exhalation, say the words in your mind:

This is me, breathing.

2

If stress is building up and you find yourself without an opportunity to vent, reach for your 'valley' point. Place your hand flat on a surface, palm down. Find the acupressure point at the base of the 'V' in the firm piece of skin between the thumb and first finger. Press firmly for up to a minute to activate the body's natural de-stressing action.

3

Some sounds are naturally relaxing. The *bija*, or 'seed', mantras are primal sounds that are said to resonate with us, connecting us to our body's energy centres, or chakras. They include sounds such as OM (pronounced 'ohm') and LAM. Find a comfortable spot and play around with simple sounds, or simply hum with your mouth closed. Place your hand on your chest, and feel how the sound vibrates through it.

4

One of the main things that drains our energy is trying to do too many things at once. Give yourself permission to do just one thing at a time for one entire day. Think about the order you'll do things in, and — most importantly — schedule in plentiful time to rest, as a priority and not an afterthought.

5

Add light to this candle. Imagine the flame flickering in a darkened room as you work — meditative mind power in action.

6

Many of us spend more time meeting and considering the needs of others, than those of ourselves. For the span of one day, place one mark on the scales for each time you do something for someone else, and a mark for each time you do something for yourself. Does the balance need to be redressed?

7

Take a deep breath in and then exhale for as long as you can, until you feel that your lungs are completely empty. Do this every time there is a weight in your chest that you want to lift.

8

Make a soothing oil to smell each time you feel anxious. Add five drops each of lavender, rose and geranium oil to a small 10ml bottle or vial. Top up the rest of the bottle with sweet almond, sunflower or coconut oil. Shake to mix. Dab a drop of the oil onto pulse points and inhale deeply as often as needed.

9

Smell is one of the most powerful senses. A single sniff, and you're transported back to a summer holiday, a specific moment in childhood, a romantic event. What are your favourite smells? What memory goes with them?

10

Bring your awareness to your nose. What can you smell right here, right now? What comes in first? Second? Close one nostril and try again. Then alternate. Does it make a difference?

11

Forest smells contribute to our wellbeing – on an emotional level as well as on a chemical level. Qing Li, President of the Japanese Society of Forest Therapy, has found that 'pleasant tree smells', also called phytoncides, boost the immune system and lower blood pressure. The essential oils transmitted by evergreens, such as the cypress tree, are especially effective. What is your favourite forest scent? Here is a breathing exercise to inhale the scents of the forest. Stand in a forest or wooded area in an upright position and relax your shoulders. Breathe in for six seconds, then breathe out for six seconds. Repeat this for one minute.

12

Where do you hold your worry? For some people it's in the neck and shoulders, for others it's in the stomach or the jaw. Imagine speaking to these parts of your body with kindness and acceptance. Tell yourself that it's OK to let go of the tension, that the past is in the past and that nothing beyond the nanosecond of the 'now' exists anyway.

13

It can be helpful to tap along your ribcage with a closed fist, whenever you want to calm down or release pent-up frustration. As you do so, imagine the ball of worry or anger dissipating with each tap – like a balloon of hot water dispersing into smaller, cooler droplets, which then evaporate entirely.

14

Stop! What parts of your body are holding tension right now? Take a deep breath and let the tension go.

For energy, try breathing in for eight seconds and out for four seconds. Repeat for one minute. Your body will be energised. To calm down, do it the other way around. Try both breathing techniques and note the difference.

This yoga exercise will also fill you with energy. Breathe in and out through your nose as quickly as you can. Keep doing this for one minute and note the outcome.

15

Time seems to move faster or slower depending on the events taking place and our mood. Sometimes it feels like time stands still. Describe a good moment in your life when your inner time behaved differently from clock time.

....

....

....

....

16

All living creatures have clocks inside; biological devices controlled by genes, hormones, the cycle of day and night, and so on. Our internal clock affects our moods, desires, appetite, and energy. It's OK to be lazy sometimes and respect your natural rhythm! Think about the following:

When do you feel most energised?

Are you a morning or an evening person?

What is generally your most difficult hour?

17

Arrange a day without any commitments and let yourself become one with the natural flow of the day. Try not to look at the clock. Sleep when you feel tired; eat when you feel hungry. Try to spend time outside. Make little notes during the day about how this feels.

....

....

....

....

18

When the blossoms fall from the trees and cover the ground with
a blanket of spring confetti, the next stage begins — the phase of
spring cleaning. Out with the old; in with the new. You can also
practise spring cleaning for your mind. Which thoughts no longer
have a good reason to occupy your mind? Which can you let go?

19

'There are always flowers for those who want
to see them,' said French painter Henri Matisse.
Go outside and look for flowers along the
roadside. Bring some home to sketch or glue
here. Even better, sit outside and paint them.

20

The moon exerts a force on the earth; that's why we have tides.
Research has shown that animals behave differently depending on the
intensity of the moonlight. Since the beginning of time, people have
assigned spiritual powers to the moon and have even planned their
actions with the lunar cycle as their guide. On a night when the moon
is bright, go for a meditative walk. Take long, deep breaths and feel
empowered by the moonlight.

21

Shamans believe that all natural objects have a spirit. They also think that every human being has one or more spirit animals to protect them, help them and guide them during dreams. What animal do you feel most connected with and why?

22

Because of the lack of sunlight, young trees grow slowly in the dense forest. But that's a good thing. Due to the slow growth, they are extra-resistant to fungi and breakage by the wind. A beech tree that looks young can actually be eighty years old. A mature beech can be 200 years old! So, for a tree, old age is relative. Imagine you could grow to be 200 years old. Would you want that? What's the reason for your answer?

23

Waves are the result of the constant interaction between wind pushing and gravity pulling the water. Listen to the ocean within you, your breath like the waves lapping ashore, continually coming and going. Let your breathing take its natural course; don't try to change it. Just accept it how it is.

24

We may not be able to see wind itself, but we can see its effects. Observe a tree on a windy day. How do the branches sway back and forth? How do the leaves move? Meditate by looking at the tree and slowly breathing in and out. When your mind starts to drift off to your to-do list, bring your attention back to the tree.

25

Perform a cloud meditation by lying on your back and watching the clouds drifting by. Realise that everything is moving: the clouds you are looking at, the earth you are resting on. Feel gravity pulling you down.

26

Stop the rush! Don't forget to take a moment for yourself on a workday. When you're on your way from A to B and you're stressed and worried, take a side route through the park and stop for a couple of minutes. You can always spare two minutes. Sit down and listen. Keep your senses active. Can you hear the grass grow? Write down what else you notice.

27

Silence and tranquility foster creativity and clear thinking. Go out into nature, sit in it for a while, and be silent.

28

Before you start an activity, any activity, focus briefly on your breathing. End the activity with a moment to focus again on your breathing, learning to tune in to the quality of the breath. Doodle some flowers in this space while concentrating on your breathing.

29

To take it slowly, we could look at the tortoise for inspiration. Never in a rush, slowly moving his legs one by one. When they're threatened, they just take shelter in their bony shell. You don't need to be fast when you are that strong. What do you gain by moving fast? Can you get where you need to be by moving slower?

30

A frog is the perfect example when meditating, according to mindfulness therapist Eline Snel, author of *Sitting Still Like a Frog*. The frog can make huge jumps, but it can also sit particularly still. It notices what is happening around it, but does not respond immediately. It breathes and sits still. Its belly bulbs up and sinks again. And what the frog can do, we can also, says Snel. Sit still like a frog and make notes afterwards.

CHAPTER 10

Be Present

Peace pilgrim and activist Satish Kumar believes that one of the most powerful things we can do to live a happier life is to aim to spend eighty per cent of our time in the present, fifteen per cent in the future and only five per cent in the past. How much time do you spend with your head in the past, dwelling heavily on days that are now behind you, or in the future — thinking about what it is you need to do, where you need to go or how you'll achieve everything on your list — rather than simply resting in the here and now, living one moment of your life at a time? It can be a sobering exercise... but a hugely empowering one too, because when we truly wake up to the power of now, absolutely everything changes. From the insistent ping of the smartphone to the ever-glow of the screen, how do we step away from non-stop 'life' for long enough to remember who, why and how we really are, and what matters most to us? Many of us are too distracted to sit with these questions for very long. We are so used to keeping ourselves busy! Yet, in the process, we have forgotten the crucial importance of doing nothing. Boredom — that particular phenomenon that social media has almost eradicated overnight with its endless stream of addictive distraction — is, in fact, a crucial component for creativity. Numerous studies have shown that letting the mind wander, having long periods of doing 'nothing' and switching off from all screens and activities, can unlock enormous potential in our minds. The next time you reach for your phone out of habit or boredom — try something new: nothing at all. Or, if that's a bridge too far, this chapter contains thirty ideas to help you do a little less, and live a whole lot more.

1

Set aside two hours of screen-free time in your diary and create a self-care intention right here, for what you'll do instead.

....

....

....

....

....

....

2

Although we might think that social media relaxes us, our brains are constantly activated by it, leaving us more tired in the end. Think of a plan to create 'white spaces' in your life – places and times without electronic devices to distract you. Note three possible white spaces:

1 ....

....

2 ....

....

3 ....

....

3

The blue light that our phones and computers emit keeps us awake and prevents our brains from producing the hormones that we need to fall asleep. Switch off all screens an hour before you go to sleep. Do something offline instead. Think of three things to do:

1 ....

2 ....

3 ....

4

Mindful doodling: fill this space with spirals; don't leave any white spaces. Try to focus only on your hand on the paper. If your mind starts to wander, bring it back to the page. Spiral away!

5

Looking into the distance is relaxing not only for your soul but also for your eyes. We look at our computer and phone screens so much that we can develop problems with our eyes. Get up at least every two hours when sitting at a screen and rest your eyes for a couple of minutes by looking into the distance. Notice the difference in your eye and facial muscles when focusing on something far away.

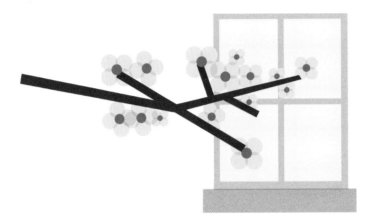

6

Neuroscientists have discovered that multitasking doesn't really exist; we are only ever sequel-tasking, switching from one task to the other and tiring our brain along the way. We try to be more efficient, but in fact we're not. Think about what tasks you are always combining. Try slowing down your pace, one thing at a time. Experiment with committing to the task you're completing before moving to the next.

7

Do nothing for two minutes.

8

When travelling by train or as a vehicle passenger, we see the world passing us by, landscapes changing from urban to rural to urban. All those transitions foster the meandering of the mind. Leave your phone in your bag and listen to your thoughts instead. Make notes of everything that comes to mind as you look at the world passing by.

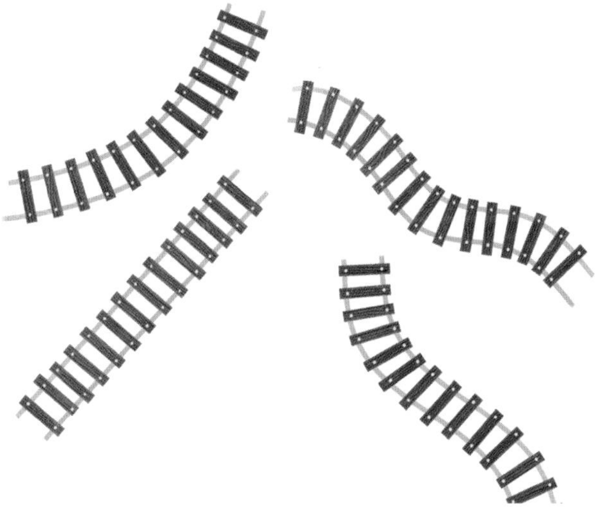

9

When was the last time you were so immersed in a creative activity that you lost all track of time? It's called 'flow' when the act you engage in absorbs your whole focus; the root of joy. Do more of it.

10

Let your mind loose with a 'wonder word search'. Fill the grid with ten words that describe you, then enter random letters in the other squares. Come back to this page on a day when you need reminding of your inherent wonder and complete the word search. Colour in your 'wonder words' in the brightest ink.

11

Breathe in for four seconds, then out for four seconds. While breathing in, draw four circles; while breathing out, change them into smileys. Repeat a few breathing cycles until this space is full.

12

In Sanskrit, mandala means 'circle' and these intricate circular patterns symbolise our own inherent 'completeness': we are all whole and we are all one. Used as meditation tools, mandalas are beautiful to draw yourself. To get you in the mood, let your pens loose on these beautiful mandalas.

13

Peace activist and writer Satish Kumar created the Pilgrim's Formula as a guide for contentment. It is where we live five per cent in the past, fifteen per cent in the future, and eighty per cent in the present moment. This is where most children live — it comes naturally. Consider how you can re-frame your focus and thoughts to move closer to this joy-supporting formula.

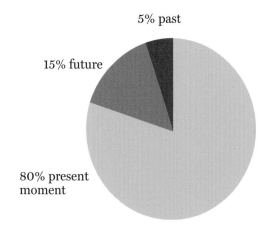

5% past

15% future

80% present moment

14

There are many more ways to look at the time than just by seeing the minutes tick by on the clock. The Greeks made a distinction between *chronos*, the time measured, and *kairos*, the 'right time' to seize the moment. *Kairos* is not about 'having' time; it's about making time. Think of something you love doing, then take a break from *chronos* and lose yourself in the activity.

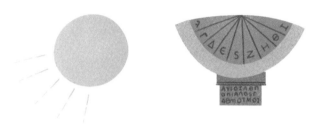

15

Colour is a visible form of energy created by light at different wavelengths and frequencies. That's why some people believe that we not only see colours, but can also feel them. Fill this space with a colour you're drawn to right now. Focus on this colour for a couple of minutes, while breathing in and out slowly, and notice how it makes you feel.

16

Humans perceive green as a neutral colour, and that's why it's relaxing for us to see. It's even been shown to improve reading ability and creativity. Go for a walk in a nearby park and notice all the different shades of green. Note how you feel before and after your walk.

....

....

....

....

....

17

Even looking at a painting or photograph of green scenery can lower your blood pressure. Collect images to make a hidden nature mood board inside a kitchen cabinet. Every time you open it, it will lift your spirits.

18

One of the wonders of nature is the way that things grow. A nautilus shell spirals in precisely the same way as a tornado — a logarithmic spiral. Even without knowing the math, it's fascinating to recognise the same shapes in different things. Look for more spirals in nature and draw one.

19

In nature, growing can sometimes mean transforming completely. The way caterpillars turn into butterflies, for example, is a magical natural phenomenon. It reminds us that every successful plan has phases: a phase of binge-eating (the research or preparation before starting); a time to go into your cocoon and work, work, work; and a time to break out of the cocoon and enjoy the flight. Write down the stages of a plan for something you want to do.

20

Colour in this technicolour butterfly as a reminder of the feeling you want to shake off today, then vigorously flap your arms and body to release the sensation from your physical being.

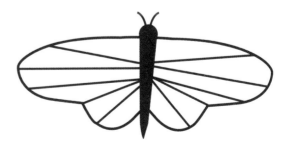

21

Why do we calm down when we splash water over our faces? It's because the action triggers the mammalian diving reflex. The body thinks that it's going for a swim underwater, so your heart rate drops — making you feel less anxious. Try it and note the difference before and after.

....

....

....

....

22

If you see a river as a metaphor for time, and you are standing at a point that is now, is the future upstream or downstream? Most people would probably say downstream because that's where the water is heading. In Paolo Cognetti's *The Eight Mountains*, the narrator's father has a different view — the future lies upstream because that is what is coming your way. Note your reflections on water as a metaphor for time.

....

....

....

....

....

....

....

23

Draw a wild ocean with big waves. Add one small boat on the water. The waves are your thoughts. The boat is you. When meditating, you become a submarine. The wild waves are above your head; they are there, but they don't affect you.

24

When things get really chaotic around you, the tornado meditation might help. A tornado is caused by differences in air pressure, which make the air move. At the outer edges of a tornado, the pressure is high, with the air in motion sweeping everything off its feet. But no matter how destructive a tornado is, in the centre there is complete silence. Find the silence inside yourself when everything around you is in motion.

25

Sit up straight and take a couple of deep breaths. Park your thoughts and to-do lists for a second. Close your eyes and concentrate on the crown of your head, then your neck and then the vertebrae down your back. Visualise your body as an extension of the earth. Imagine that you cling to the earth, and that you let all your stress and worries flow into it.

26

Perform a mountain meditation. Close your eyes and think of a mountain. Imagine you are that mountain. You are thousands of years old; you are huge and rise above everything else. Everything happening to you is just temporary and leaves you untouched.

27

Pick a daily task and do it in slow motion. Notice what happens with your thoughts as well as your execution of the task.

28

Inhale deeply. What can you smell right now? Try to focus on a different scent with every inhalation.

29

Scheduling time to do nothing is easier if you have a clearer view of what you spend (or waste!) your time on. Estimate how long you spend on every element of your life — friends, family, phone, a hobby, commuting, running errands, work — and draw a pie chart on a piece of paper to illustrate the balance of your life.

30

Meditate for at least five minutes. Tip to help you focus: notice the difference between air coming in and air going out when breathing.

CHAPTER 11

Prioritise Healing

Human beings are incredible — inherently resilient, innovative and adaptable. We have so much to be proud of — we learnt how to make fire and invented the wheel, after all. Yet there are countless times in our lives when we let our own self-limiting beliefs sneak in and fool us into suspecting that we aren't as good as we ought to be, times when we let comparison, doubt and fear steal our magical thunder and hold us back from living the life we want. Yes, we all have our fair share of dirty laundry — stuff that's been hanging around for years: regrets, memories, fear, guilt. No one is immune from making mistakes, but there is no shame in this. The 'beginner's mind', a Zen Buddhist ideology, refers to the open, receptive, ever-learning state of being that accepts we are not experts (and are never going to be), that we are all eternal students, here to experience life moment by moment without set expectations or rigid mindsets. Isn't that freeing? To realise that wherever we come from, whatever we have done and however many mistakes we fear we have made in our lives, that not one of us is immune from the opportunity to move on and move forward. Here, we reclaim our joy by getting out of our own way, by renouncing our need to be always right and by understanding that the more fixed our mindset is, the more limited our potential becomes. Carrying around a lifetime of guilt, worry, fear and regret? This is where you can sketch out and doodle down all of those perceived imperfections and inconsistencies. Clear the air once and for all.

1

Choose three words that describe who you really are beneath the baggage, obligations, worries and requirements. Who are 'you' at your very core? Write your three words here.

2

Find two photographs of yourself; one in which you are completely relaxed and at home in your body, being kind to and accepting of yourself, and the other where you are self-conscious and lacking in confidence. Look closely into the eyes of the 'you' who felt both things. What comes up?

3

People across many cultures, use fire as a symbol of new beginnings. On paper scraps, write down three things you no longer want to carry into the next cycle of your life; throw them into a real fire.

1 ....

2 ....

3 ....

4

Sometimes, sacrifices are well worth making. Think back on a time when you put everything on the line, or gave up something important, and gained something better as a result. Remind yourself that sometimes you must leave things behind in order to get where you need to go.

5

Silver linings abound all around, even on the darkest days. Consider something that has caused you pain or discomfort in the past year. Now, feel into what you may have learnt from this challenge. Don't overthink it — simply write down whatever comes up for you. Read over your words. How does that feel?

6

Begin writing a new diary entry where all of the negative narratives from the past year work out wonderfully well in the end. Keep coming back and adding to it each time you imagine twists and turns in your own happily ending tale.

7

Courage is not fearlessness – it is feeling the
fear and doing it anyway. Award yourself this
medal for bravery. Mark it with a time you
faced – and conquered – your fear.

8

Fill this trophy cabinet with all the times you felt most joyful, free and at
peace in yourself. Let this be what you celebrate, irrespective of outcome.

9

Do you always have to be right? Or do you find it hard to speak up at all?
Use this mind map to confront a time when you should have walked away
from an argument for the peace of your own mind. Or, use it to confront a
time when you should have argued your point. How did you feel? What do you
wish you had done differently? What can you learn from revisiting it?

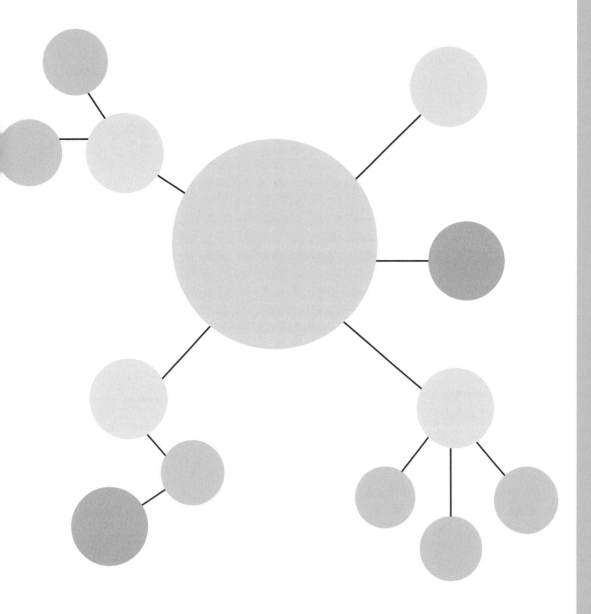

10

The more we practise positive thinking, the more it sticks. What's your perpetual pet peeve? How can you reframe it? Is there a funny side? Use this perspective-o-meter to draw your peeve at the size it really is in comparison to the enormity of a life-or-death concern. Give your peeve another look... has it shrunk in importance?

11

Saying something out loud can help shift the perspective of it. If you're upset about something, talk about it out loud to yourself right now. Listen to yourself as though you were listening to a best friend. Without labouring over it, write down the advice you'd give.

12

What promise did you make to yourself recently that you failed to keep? Write it down and re-make it, setting a date and time when you can follow through.

13

Remember, in the words of George Eliot, that it is never too late to be who you might have been. What lights up your soul? What excites you? What do you feel most impassioned and motivated by? Make that the seed of your next project.

14

Many of us hold on to things that weigh us down — from the scratchy shirt we never feel comfortable in to old photographs from troubling times. Fill these lines with the things you no longer need and then cross them out to cut them loose.

15

It's estimated that from all the thoughts we have in one day (and that's a lot), only twenty per cent are new. Have a critical look at your thoughts and think of which you might be repeating over and over. Write some here.

16

The beliefs we hold about ourselves define us in many ways. What beliefs might be holding you back? Write them down here.

....

....

....

....

....

....

....

....

....

....

....

....

....

17

Against each self-limiting belief you wrote in the previous activity, write one way in which you have already disproven it... or intend to. Remember, thoughts are just thoughts; they are not facts.

....

....

....

....

....

....

....

....

....

....

....

....

18

How often do we say 'I can't do this', and then do it anyway? Have fun crossing out these joy-stealing space invaders. Every time you cancel out an 'I can't', replace it with an 'I can!'.

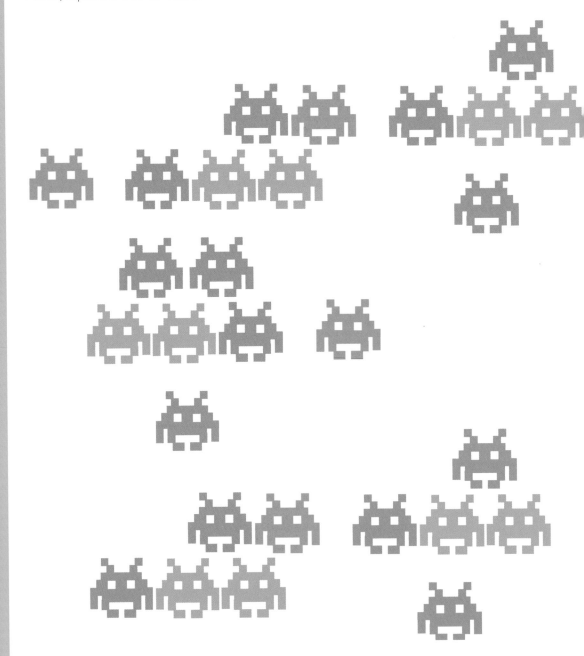

19

We all have an inner critic telling us that what we make isn't good enough.
Give your inner critic a face by drawing it here. Then lock it up by drawing
bars over it and throwing away the key.

20

There's an old saying that when the gods wish to punish us, they grant our wishes. What things have you dreamt of, only to realise they are not as wonderful as you imagined them to be? Do not chastise yourself — we are all made to have wants and aspirations — but we are, in fact, most content when we fully cherish all that we already have. Begin where you are.

Remember that even the gods get it wrong sometimes. What dreams have you had that have come true and brought great joy with them? Celebrate them here.

21

Ferns are true survivors. They grow almost everywhere and they've been around for millions of years. Young fern leaves start out curled up in a ball. When they grow, they slowly unroll. It's beautiful to see. When have you felt yourself unfurling and growing?

22

Making a weather report of your current mood and emotions is a well-known mindfulness practice. What's the weather like inside your head? Is it cloudy? Is it sunny? Do you feel a thunderstorm coming? Note or draw your own little symbols for how you're feeling right now.

23

Just like waves and clouds, difficult times will come and go. Add washes
of colour to this fleeting, changeable scene as a reminder of the inherent
impermanence of everything.

24

All our emotions resonate in the body, but most of the time we are too disconnected to notice. Think of something that upsets you. Try to notice where in your body you feel your emotions.

25

'People who dare to be vulnerable in relationships are the happiest,' says American researcher and writer Brené Brown. Not being ashamed of your weaknesses and not covering them up is the key to real human connection. What are the weaknesses you would rather hide from people? When do you feel vulnerable? Who do you feel safe with?

26

The loss of precious connections can be devastating, but we keep our loved ones alive in our hearts and in our memories. Write a postcard to a loved one who has passed away and draw a picture on the front that connects you to each other.

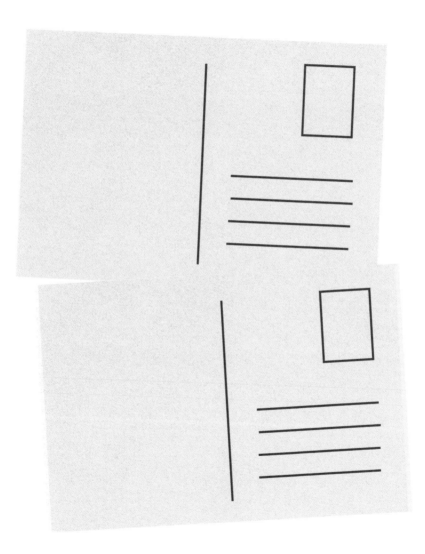

27

People love helping others most of the time, but asking for help is one of the hardest things. In what area would you like help in your life? Write a message reaching out for help. Consider passing it on to someone who might be able to give you what you need.

28

Everyone has a special gift... but some people need a little more help in locating it. Imagine that you are talking to a best friend. What would they say to you when you express a lack of talent? List your pep talk points down here.

29

Outside of your comfort zone is where most of the magic happens. It's where you find unexpected beauty; it's where you learn that you are capable of more than you think; it's where you meet new people; it's where you create amazing things, with great stories to tell. Recall a moment when you were completely out of your comfort zone and something beautiful happened.

30

Doing nothing can also mean accepting a situation as it is, and not trying to change it. Think of three things in your life that you want to change, but can't at the moment. Can you let go?

1

2

3

CHAPTER 12

Have Fun

Adulting isn't always all it's cracked up to be. Even for those who live a relatively low-key life, we must still navigate our collective eco-anxiety and global social political unrest and uncertainty. The cumulative effect of life's daily challenges — exacerbated by, among other things, 24/7 connectivity and technology — has brought many of us to the point where we feel continually overwhelmed and constantly stressed. And this is why we need a monumentally magnificent dose of joy to mitigate it! There is nothing more life-affirming than joy — joy that roots itself down into the foundations of real life and sprouts up, blooming and beautiful, through every seam of our everyday fabric. Here, in this chapter, we take our lead from children, who are naturally joyous, curious and freespirited. We remember how to learn through play, where every day is a rich, enjoyable adventure. Though it is not easy to free ourselves from years of being told to grow up and stop being so silly, there is ample research to show that having a playful state of mind not only reduces stress levels, but also makes us more creative and adaptable in our responses and solutions to stressful situations. In fact 'play' is quite possibly the most underrated pastime of all, as it leads to improved wellbeing, better relationships, increased longevity and a better night's sleep, among other things. Here, we banish the rules and regulations and the to-do lists, and just return to some good old-fashioned fun. From the simple joy of a good tongue twister to the naughtiest tricks we ever played, this chapter is filled with celebratory ways to coax out your inner kid.

1

What enjoyable activities have you not tried since childhood? Skipping? Using a hula hoop? Playing hopscotch? Set an intention to revisit one childhood activity a month. That's reclaiming joy in action!

2

Make a toe-tapping playlist of the songs you simply cannot sit still to. Listen to it when everyone else around you is still and stoney-faced (on a commuter train or in a traffic jam, perhaps). Imagine everyone bursting into a crescendo of song and dance. Smiles all round.

3

Illustrate the first letter of your name in the most beautiful, colourful way possible, just as you would find letters in old fairy tale books.

4

Do you remember the riotous fun you had as a kid, when tasked with devising a new invention? If you could invent one thing now, what would it be? From the unlimited-ice-cream machine to a rucksack-jetpack, let your mind run free. Doodle your ideas here.

5

Etch a house into this majestic tree. Fill your imagination with the mischief you'll get up to, up and away in your own private arboreal abode.

6

Trace a favourite phrase or word that makes you smile onto this steamed-up bathroom mirror.

7

Have fun solving this word code with a beginner's mind. Ask yourself, 'I wonder how this works?' Take as long as you need. No prizes for winning — only trying. Only three of the following four words has a number code. If the letters correspond to numbers, what is the number code for the word MUSE? You'll find the answer on page 200.

SWUM

FERN

WEST

TRUE

7236

1687

8139

8

Living life in full technicolour means never dimming your own personality, but living your whole, unapologetic truth. Fill in this swatch chart with your heart and soul's boldest colours. Then give every colour a name that is unique and meaningful to you.

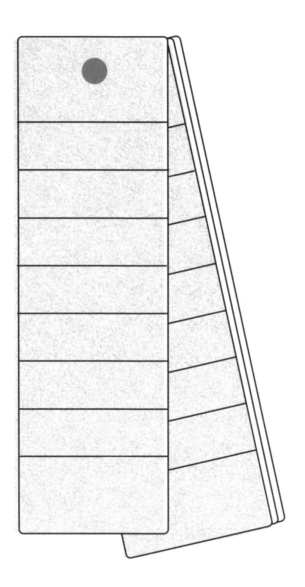

9

We might all do well to take a leaf out of a child's book. Close your eyes and re-imagine yourself as a kid, wild and free, marching to the beat of your own drum. Hold that feeling in your heart!

10

Make time over the coming months to start your own joy box. If you have memories and mementos scattered about your home, gather any you do not wish to display. Find, decorate or repurpose a box in a way that encapsulates joy for you. Take great joy in adding to your box each and every time something touches your heart.

11

What craft did you enjoy most at school? Making collages or papier mâché? Knitting or woodwork? Watercolours or appliqué? Add touches of your lost arts to your joy box — whether directly to the box itself or stored within — as an ongoing project to pick up on rainy days.

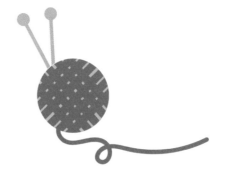

Answer to 7: 4386

12

Revisit a favourite childhood story. Read it just as you would have read it as a child – make a den, create a cosy corner or crawl under the covers with a torch.

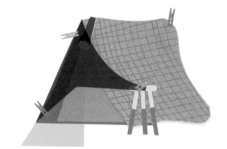

13

Planes flying overhead always come with rich and imaginative adventure stories. Where is this plane going? Who's onboard? What happens once they arrive?

14

Children are often chided with 'look, don't touch', but their urge to hold and feel things is intrinsic to learning. We often realise things about objects only when we hold them – a soft, fluffy thing may feel surprisingly rough, while a scaled, leathery surface might be deliciously soft. Move around your home, or outside space, picking up objects at random. Learn their secrets as you cup them in your hands.

15

Have fun saying these three devilishly tricky tongue twisters out loud, speeding up with each repetition. Challenge your friends for bonus joy.

The sixth sick sheik's sheep's sick.

Betty Botter bought some butter but she said the butter's bitter if I put it in my batter, it will make my batter bitter but a bit of better butter will make my batter better so 'twas better Betty Botter bought a bit of better butter.

A tutor who tooted the flute tried to tutor two tooters to toot. Said the two to the tutor, 'Is it harder to toot or to tutor two tooters to toot?'

16

Did you ever have a special 'spell' you'd repeat as a child? Something to comfort you or make you feel powerful, or to change what was happening around you? Write down the words that come to you now.

17

When you were a child, too young to know about careers, what did you aspire to be? A unicorn? An explorer? A superhero? Sketch out your childhood hero or heroine here.

18

Unbelievably, 242 words can be made from the word UNBELIEVABLE!
Challenge yourself to come up with as many as you can over time.

Unbelievable

19

What was the most mischievous thing you did as a kid? Re-live it here, guilt-free.

20

Flash fiction is hugely entertaining — a super-short story, in which an entire world is encapsulated in just a few hundred words. Don't waste time or words on the introduction, but begin right in the middle of the story, choose every word wisely and make sure the final line packs a punch. Off you go...

21

Beginning on the 'start dot', complete an impromptu, unplanned drawing, without lifting your pencil from the page until you reach the 'end dot'.

Start

● End

22

Add details to this rosette and award it to your inner kid for making it through another day with a hearty dose of fun and frolics.

23

Time for some succulent love. Give this cute
cactus the full colour treatment.

24

Play can be as simple as finding the unusual in things that
are familiar and finding joy in the mundane – words, for
example, are an endless source of play.

Invent a new word by putting two words together. It can be
so refreshing to do something that has no use whatsoever.

25

It's time for an old game of 'dots and boxes' with someone. Simple games like this are a fun way to relax and reconnect. Using a different coloured pen or pencil each, take it in turns to draw a line between two horizontally or vertically adjacent dots. Whoever is first to complete the fourth side of a square, colours in the box they have created and draws another line. The player with the most boxes in their colour at the end of the game wins.

26

The human mind is a connection machine. Challenge your creativity with a little game of associations. Start with the word 'play' then write the first word you associate with it. After that, write a word you associate with the second word, and so on. Write as many words as you can in two minutes.

Play

27

Draw as if you are a five-year-old.

28

Make your day into a tiny cartoon.

29

Design the front cover of a book you might write one day.

30

Playing keeps you young at heart. Next time you pass a playground, try one of the swings and swing like a seven-year-old. How high can you go?

Conclusion

So… you've arrived at the end of the book. But what about you? Where do you find yourself? A question that's also very happy to be taken literally. Try it — look around you. What do you see? Hear? Smell? Is there a taste on your tongue? What do you feel beneath or through the parts of your body that are in contact with any other surfaces? How does this 'tuning in' to your environment, position, sensations, change your relationship with the thoughts you were having before, or the feelings that may have arisen since?

This practice — a continual, habitual bringing of the mind back to the moment, and the gentle landing of your thoughts, feelings and focus, back into your body — is, we hope, one that has become a little (or perhaps even a lot) easier as you've travelled through this book. It's not always easy to remain mindful in a world that can feel increasingly mindless, which is why these daily micro-habits and sparks of inspiration are so important. A slow drip-drip-drip of water will still, eventually, fill the cup. Likewise, the tortoise beats the hare not through force or power or speed, but simply because it perseveres: slow and steady wins the race.

And, perhaps, this book has also inspired you to do just a few little things slightly differently. Or perhaps it's sparked a sea change at home, or in the way you nourish yourself, or the choices you make about the natural world around you. All of these choices are taking you in the right direction. They are the drip-drip-drip that becomes a daily life filled with meaningful rituals and helpful habits.

Even if some of your habits have floundered and you've not quite managed to make the good stuff really 'stick' just yet — that's more than OK. Because what you've done simply by being here — being open to new ideas, trying something different, learning a new skill or sharing a fun fact — matters too, more than anything, and anything is possible.

FURTHER RESOURCES

BOOKS ABOUT HAPPINESS, PLAY & FLOW

The Joy Journal for Magical Everyday Play: Easy Activities & Creative Craft for Kids and their Grown-ups, Laura Brand (Bluebird, 2020)

Play: How It Shapes the Brain, Opens the Imagination, and Invigorates the Soul, Stuart Brown M.D. (Penguin, 2010)

Flow, The Psychology of Optimal Experience, Mihaly Csikszentmihalyi (HarperCollins, 2008)

Man's Search for Meaning, Viktor E. Frankl (Beacon Press, 2019)

Joyful: The Surprising Power of Ordinary Things to Create Extraordinary Happiness, Ingrid Fetell Lee (Rider, 2018)

Happiness: Essential Mindfulness Practices, Thich Nhat Hanh (Parallax Press, 2009)

Michael Rosen's Book of Play: Why Play Really Matters, and 101 Ways to Get More of it in Your Life, Michael Rosen (Wellcome Collection, 2019)

Play the Forest School Way: Woodland Games, Crafts and Skills for Adventurous Kids Book, Jane Worroll and Peter Houghton (Watkins Publishing, 2008)

BOOKS ABOUT NATURE & SELF-SUFFICIENCY

If Women Rose Rooted: A Life-changing Journey to Authenticity and Belonging, Sharon Blackie (September Publishing, 2019)

100 Things to do in a Forest, Jennifer Davis and Eleanor Taylor (Laurence King Publishing, 2020)

Trees, Leaves, Flowers & Seeds: Visual Encyclopedia of the Plant Kingdom, DK and The Smithsonian Institution (DK, 2019)

Braiding Sweetgrass: Indigenous Wisdom, Scientific Knowledge and the Teachings of Plants, Robin Wall Kimmerer (Penguin, 2020)

Food for Free, Richard Mabey (Collins, 2012)

The New Complete Book of Self-Sufficiency: the Classic Guide for Realists and Dreamers, John Seymour (DK, 2019)

Self-Sufficiency: Foraging for Wild Foods, David Squire (IMM Lifestyle, 2015)

Practical Self-Sufficiency: the Complete Guide to Sustainable Living Today, Dick Strawbridge and James Strawbridge (DK, 2020)

BOOKS ABOUT CREATIVITY & STORYTELLING

The Story Cure: An A-Z of Books to Keep Kids Happy, Healthy and Wise, Ella Berthould and Susan Elderkin (Canongate, 2016)

The Artist's Way: A Spiritual Path to Higher Creativity, Julia Cameron (Souvenir Press, 2020)

Big Magic: How to Live a Creative Life and Let Go of Your Fear, Elizabeth Gilbert (Bloomsbury, 2016)

The Storytelling Animal: How Stories Make Us Human, Jonathan Gottshcall (Houghton Mifflin Harcourt USA, 2013)

Creative Confidence: Unleashing the Creative Potential within Us All, David Kelley and Tom Kelley (HarperCollins, 2015)

The Lost Words and The Lost Spells, Robert Macfarlane and Jackie Morris (Hamish Hamilton, 2020)

Creatrix: She Who Makes, Lucy H Pearce (Womancraft Publishing, 2019)

Daemon Voices: Essays on Storytelling, Philip Pullman (David Fickling Books, 2017)

WEBSITE

Action for Happiness

actionforhappiness.org

Project Happiness

projecthappiness.org

The Conscious Kid

theconsciouskid.org

The Happiness Research Institute

happinessresearchinstitute.com

The Happy Newspaper

thehappynewspaper.com

MAGAZINES

Flow

flowmagazine.com

Juno

junomagazine.com

Resurgence

resurgence.org/magazine

The Green Parent

thegreenparent.co.uk

ABOUT THE AUTHORS

Emine Kali Rushton is the former Wellness Director of Psychologies magazine, and former Editor of oh magazine and in her 20 years in editorial, has written for numerous titles, including The ST Style, Harper's Bazaar, ELLE, NYLON, iD, JUNO and The Green Parent. She is also the author of five books, including *Natural Wellness Every Day*, *SATTVA: The Ayurvedic Way to Live Well*, and *Reclaim Joy*. She is a qualified holistic therapist, and is presently studying Herbal Medicine. She lives in Kent where she runs The Clearing with her family — a membership space for those who want to live in harmony with nature and the seasons.

Jocelyn de Kwant is a journalist and editor specialising in nature, mindfulness and simple living. She is the author of two books: *Creative Flow* and *Nature Tonic*. These last few years, Jocelyn changed course and studied ecology and nature conservation. She recently started working as a forester in the Netherlands.